An Introduction to
Crewel Embroidery

An Introduction to
Crewel Embroidery

Mave Glenny

Guild of Master Craftsman Publications Ltd

First published 1998 by
Guild of Master Craftsman Publications Ltd,
166 High Street, Lewes,
East Sussex BN7 1XU

© Mavis Glenny 1998

Reprinted 1999

ISBN 1 86108 084 0

Photography by Esler Crawford
Line drawings by Simon Rodway

Designed by Fineline Studios
Typeface: Palatino
Colour reproduction by Job Color srl–Gorle (BG)–Italy
Printed in Hong Kong by H&Y Printing Ltd

Contents

DON'T BE IMPRESSED WITH WHAT I HAVE ACHIEVED. IT HAS COME ABOUT THROUGH THE GRACE OF GOD THAT HAS BEEN AT WORK IN ME.

Selwyn Hughes, *Every Day With Jesus,*
November/December 1996

Acknowledgements

I owe special thanks to the following people who, in their own way, each contributed to the writing of this book: to my husband Lee, for his faith in my ability, his patience, encouragement and practical support; to my friend Helen Johnston, for her thoughtfulness and sense of humour; to my friends John and Heather Cole, for their generosity and support; to Esler Crawford, for his care over the photographs; to the Sheldon Gallery in Newtownards for kindly lending frames and offering advice; to Appleton's for freely supplying threads; and lastly but by no means leastly, my dear Mother who, many years ago, ignited the initial spark and inspired me to stitch.

Measurements

Although care has been taken to ensure that metric measurements are true and accurate, they are only conversions from imperial. Throughout the book instances may be found where a metric measurement has slightly varying imperial equivalents, because in each particular case the closest convenient equivalent has been given. **Care should be taken to use either imperial or metric measurements consistently.** (See also Metric Conversion Table, page 99.)

Introduction

Over the centuries, many differing styles and techniques of embroidery and needlecraft have evolved and our present-day crafts are all drawn from this wealth of tradition.

Embroidery is one of the most versatile art forms of all time. Its versatility becomes even more apparent through all the wonderful varieties of threads and fabrics so readily available today. During the past few years cross stitch, tapestry and patchwork have undergone a resurgence of interest and are now popular pastimes once again. Sadly, this has left the more skilful art of freehand embroidery lagging behind. Hand embroidery has to some extent been manoeuvred into the background by modern technology. I use the word 'manoeuvred' because it conjures up the images of man, manufacture and machines, which have all, in their own way, played their part in devaluing the work of the creative hand embroiderer. This, I feel, is a great pity, especially as so much more individual creativity can be utilized in freehand embroidery.

There are various styles of hand embroidery, but I have been exploring the style known as 'crewel' embroidery, trying to bring it up to date by using a modern approach. The variations in wool colours, in texture and design, and the uses that can be found for this style of embroidery are endless.

The projects, designs and techniques outlined in this book can be used by the beginner or the more experienced embroiderer. The Stitch Dictionary (see pages 81–96) gives simple written instructions as well as diagrams for the beginner and will no doubt refresh the memory of the more seasoned embroiderer. There are projects to suit everyone's taste. For the beginner the best starting point might be the stitch sampler, the ceramic bowl lid, the leaf and flower design, or the spectacle case. The slightly more adventurous might begin with the circular floral design, the tulip design, the cushion covers or the placemat and tablecloth design. For those who like a challenge, the galleon picture, writing pad case, bell pull and butterfly box will offer scope for developing their skills further.

Whichever projects you choose, I trust that they will be the inspiration needed for you to use your own creative talents and that you will be surprised and amazed with the results you can achieve. Happy stitching.

Chapter One

History and Development

Although the exact date and origins of the first crewel embroideries have proved very elusive, it is believed that the technique came on the scene around the fifteenth century or earlier.

Crewel work is a type of embroidery using two-ply woollen yarn, which is worked both on and above the surface of the material, by layering stitches up over each other, either in a set format (see Battlement Couching in the Stitch Dictionary, page 81) or randomly, to achieve the desired effect. The particular variety of two-ply worsted woollen yarn used is known as 'crewel' and gives the style of embroidery its name. The word 'crewel' is thought to be derived from the Anglo-Saxon word *cleow* meaning 'ball of thread'. It is believed these crewel yarns were also used in earlier times for making tapestries and lace.

Crewel stitches fall into four main groups which are derived from back, running, and knot or coral, or loop stitches (see Stitch Dictionary, pages 81–96). The versatility of these stitches, and the subtle colour variations of the yarns, gives great scope to the creative embroiderer. Many other 'freestyle' embroidery stitches may also be used for crewel work.

Early influences

Although crewel work itself may only have been in vogue for approximately five centuries, embroidery using woollen yarn goes back much further than that, particularly in Britain and France. One of the earliest known is what is commonly called the 'Bayeux Tapestry', dating back over 900 years. In fact, this is not a tapestry at all but a woollen embroidery worked on coarse linen, depicting the Battle of Hastings. Just eight colours were employed, namely terracotta, buff, yellow, two blues and three greens. The Tapestry is believed to have been commissioned by Bishop Odo of Bayeux for the cathedral, dedicated in 1077. Its survival may well be due to the hard-wearing and tough nature of the linen and to the fact that the wool embroidery could not easily be recycled for any other use.

Jacobean influences

Today, crewel work is sometimes mistakenly called 'Jacobean work', from the style of design which developed in the seventeenth century and which remains a major influence in more modern crewel work. Influences upon design in that era may be attributed to two main sources: the characteristic Tudor emphasis on floral shapes and the Far Eastern styles which were assimilated following the increase in trade of exotic goods from India and China that flowed from the formation of the East India Company by London merchants. Two typical Jacobean crewel work motifs are shown in Fig 1.1.

Fig 1.1 The patterns for two typical Jacobean shapes used in crewel work.

The embroideries in Jacobean times developed what is known as the 'tree of life' design (see below). This consists chiefly of rather unnatural-looking leaves and floral forms on a central, tree-like growth, rising from rounded hillocks. A variety of somewhat quaint animals and birds were also introduced into the designs, with rabbits, squirrels, deer, peacocks and birds of paradise being to the fore. Then, from the flower beds of England came further influences in the form of flowers, including the rose as the national emblem, the carnation, which was the symbol of the Stuart family, and honeysuckle, marigolds, irises and the potato flower. Interspersed with these more common flowers were other more exotic varieties, often with many petals.

Popular pattern arrangements

In England, Jacobean embroidery involved three main pattern arrangements.

1 **The Tree of Life design**
   This design appears to have been taken from East Indian *palimpores* (printed cotton bed covers) and was interpreted and embroidered in many ways. The design became so popular that large hangings were later embroidered in fine chain stitch and sold in India.
2 **The Elizabethan scroll design**
   The main feature of the 'scroll' was a dominant pattern of sweeping stems, worked on a large scale, which curved around and almost enveloped the particular flowers or leaves within them. While there was

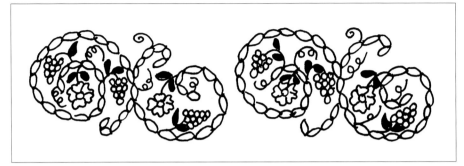

Fig 1.2 An Elizabethan scroll design.

a variation in motifs, the unifying influence was the strong dominating stem line (see Fig 1.2).

3 **A wavy border**
   This slightly later pattern consisted of a wavy border, enclosed with straight lines. This provided an area within which there were regularly sprigged small motifs.

Uses for crewel embroidery

Crewel work was mostly used for bedspreads, valances, curtains for four-poster beds and wall hangings. For the ladies there were petticoats and pockets (two of which would be tied around the waist under a dress and

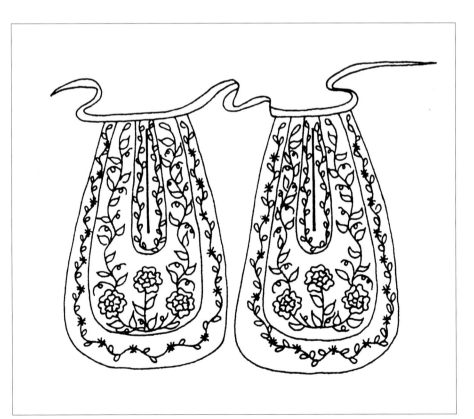

Fig 1.3 Embroidered pockets to be worn under a dress.

Fig 1.4 Details taken from Abigail Pett's bed hangings.

used for keeping small household items, see Fig 1.3). Examples of such work survive today.

The most famous of all the seventeenth-century crewel work is generally recognized as the bed hangings made by Abigail Pett (an amateur needlewoman) around 1675. On the bed curtains and valances of her vast work, no two motifs are exactly alike in colour or stitch (see Fig 1.4). The Far Eastern influence is evident in some of the more exotic birds included. These bed hangings may be seen in the Victoria and Albert Museum in London. The bed was often the most popular item of furniture to be adorned with crewel work. For example, Hampton Court records indicate that Cardinal Wolsey had 230 beds there, mostly hung with embroidery and silk.

Royalty is also associated with an interest in such embroidery. The young princesses and girls of the court were taught many different forms of embroidery alongside their other studies. Mary, Queen of Scots was a well educated and intelligent woman. She was encouraged to develop an interest in needlework by her mother-in-law, Catherine de Medici, who had learned her skill as a child in Florence. Mary darned net, and used tent stitch, cross stitch, raised work and laid work in her embroideries. She also mastered the art of making linen garments, as well as bed and table linen.

It is believed that Mary founded a school of needlework at Châteaudun in France. She employed her own designers, two of whom were Pierre Oudry and Charles Houvart. Pierre Oudry, on several occasions, was rewarded for special service beyond the drawing of her designs on to canvas. It is believed that he followed Mary to England.

Mary planned all her pieces of embroidery to be functional, and considered the design more important than the technique. During her time in prison, it is likely that Mary spent many hours working on embroidery. A white satin chasuble embroidered with silver and coloured silks is attributed to Mary, as well as a set of bed hangings at Scone Palace. The pieces of embroidery that can most confidently be regarded as Mary's work are those bearing her crowned initials or cipher. However, initials joined to the R for Regina, and crowned with the national flowers of Scotland, England and France, all bear the stamp of Mary, Queen of Scots. Most of the pieces bearing Mary's initials or cipher can be seen at Oxburgh Hall, Norfolk.

Silk influences

Around the middle of the eighteenth century, the use of silk threads came into greater prominence, with silk often being combined with wool. Silk quilted backgrounds also provided a different medium on which to work crewel embroidery. This quilted fabric tended to require more open patterns and fewer stitches and the use of bright colours highlighted the overall effect. This lighter trend in design was continued by Robert Adam for his furniture upholstery. However, crewel wool embroidery began to diminish in popularity and by the turn of the century was superseded almost entirely by silk. Nowadays crewel work is still used for large wall hangings and bedspreads, but it is also worked in finer details for such items

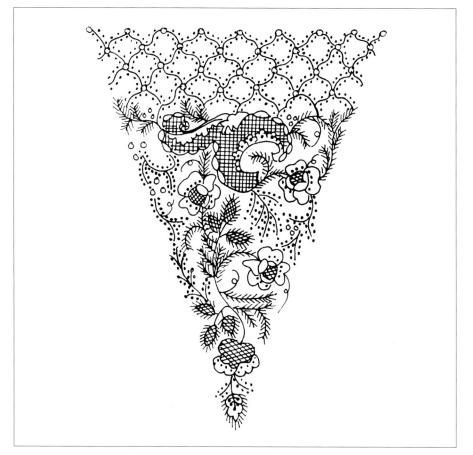

Fig 1.5 Sample of a bodice insert for a dress.

time many designs were also simplified. The 'tree of life' design was reduced to a triangle and motifs were more often detached and spaced at intervals on a plain background.

Other uses for crewel wools

In the eighteenth century, a new type of pictorial embroidery came more to the fore, particularly in England. This involved crewel wools being worked in irregular long and short stitches on a coarse canvas in a needle-painting technique. The end results were copies of oil paintings. More attractive to some modern eyes may be contemporary pictures worked both in wool and silk on taffeta grounds, in which details such as the sky and faces of figures were painted in watercolour. These pictures tended to be based on paintings and engravings of pastoral scenes and portraits by artists such as George Morland (1763–1804).

Nineteenth- and twentieth-century trends

The development of embroidery during the nineteenth century, although complex, can perhaps be highlighted by the contrasts provided by Berlin woolwork and the designs of William Morris (1834–96). The printing of designs on squared paper, forming the basis of the technique used in Berlin woolwork, was initiated by a Berlin print-seller around 1804. The soft, beautifully shaded embroidery wools were also produced in Germany

as dress inserts (see Fig 1.5) and decorative accessories.

American influences

In America the crewel fashion lasted longer. Although the first American designs inherited English influences, it was not long before certain characteristics made the American embroideries distinctive. For example, the English and East Indian designs, with animals, flowers and trees predominating, often received a radical transformation. Bed hangings, petticoats and other items were stitched by American embroiderers with more local influences such as sheep, chickens, wild grapes, pine trees and other features of a rural but developing America.

Another difference in many American designs is that they were often worked in outline, producing an effect of lightness and gaiety. Perhaps part of their appeal is that, although balanced designs were produced, they rarely have repeat motifs. The American embroiderers tended to dispense with the more orthodox stitches such as satin, herringbone, rope, coral, feather, cable and flame stitch, replacing them with romanian, buttonhole and block shading stitches and french knots. Over a period of until the 1840s. A catalogue of designs was issued, then the designs were hand-painted on to soft canvas and sent to the purchaser, ready to be worked in cross stitch.

William Morris, on the other hand, was aware that there was a need to reform and improve the quality of needlework. He was appalled that the craft and expertise of the master craftsman or -woman was being devalued by machine-made goods.

It was at the age of 36 in 1870, that William Morris began to extend his artistic and architectural skills to textile design. Morris learned to embroider (by unpicking embroideries) and then he taught his wife Jane and his two daughters. He experimented with seventeenth-century crewel work techniques and the hangings on his bed at Kelmscott Manor are fine examples of his approach to embroidery.

Inspiration for William Morris's woven textiles came from both medieval and Eastern sources (see Fig 1.6). His success in weaving textiles gave him the confidence to experiment in tapestry-weaving. Many of his wallpaper designs were also used for textiles. He was not happy using the new chemical or aniline dyes and began experimenting with natural dyes and dyeing techniques. Morris's revival of what was basically crewel embroidery helped to hasten the decline in the 1870s of the more mechanical Berlin woolwork. Most importantly, his work both as a wallpaper and textile designer did much to inspire embroiderers in his day, and continues to inspire many today.

Embroidery has battled through the twentieth century against a background of technological, economic and social changes. The introduction of mass-produced embroidery has threatened at times to extinguish the viability of the more unique and individualistic hand embroidery. Despite periods at a low ebb, however, hand embroidery has survived. At the present time many forms of hand embroidery and crafts are undergoing a revival. Men and women today are more conscious of and interested in colour, current trends in design and fashion, and the uniqueness of what they can produce by their own achievements. One bonus factor in the survival of hand embroidery may well be the sense of lasting, individual satisfaction obtained by the embroiderer on the completion of a piece of work.

It is my hope and desire that what follows in this book may in some small way rekindle the desire and enthuse many to become involved in the art of embroidery, and in particular that of crewel embroidery.

Fig 1.6 Details adapted from a William Morris wallpaper and textile design.

Chapter Two

Basic Materials and Equipment

Crewel work does not demand any complicated or prohibitively expensive equipment and materials. If you are a keen needleworker you will have all the basic equipment already, except perhaps for specialist needles and embroidery frames (see Fig 2.1). The threads and fabrics for a particular project may, of course, need to be purchased specially, or even dyed at home if you are feeling adventurous. Advice on all these points is given in this and subsequent chapters.

Equipment

Needles

Crewel or embroidery needles
These are sharp, medium-length needles with long eyes. The finest crewel needle for wool work would usually be a size 8; a useful needle for multi-purpose work is a size 5; for heavier work, or when using more than one thread at a time, a size 3 or 4 is more suitable.

Tapestry needles These blunt needles will also be needed for those stitches worked *over* the surface of the fabric. Threaded back stitch, interlaced running stitch, weaving stitch and spider's web stitch (see Stitch Dictionary) all need to be woven with a blunt needle to avoid snagging or piercing the previously formed foundation stitches.

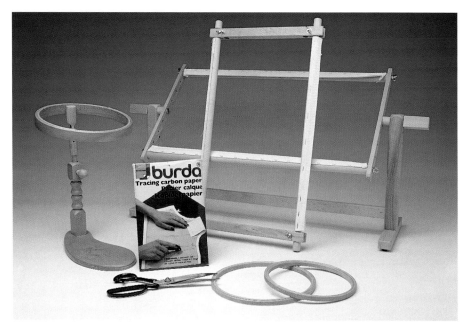

Fig 2.1 *A selection of essential equipment.*

Chenille needles A sharp, wide, long-eyed needle should be used with metallic threads. Some metallic threads are quite thick and made of synthetic fibres, twisted around a central core. Using the larger-eyed chenille needle makes threading the needle so much easier.

/ / / / / / / / / / / / / / / / / / / /
Tip **If you find threading needles difficult, cut a piece of paper which is small enough to go through the eye of the needle, but long enough to fold over the thread. Place the thread lengthwise inside the folded paper, then insert the paper and thread through the eye of the needle.**
/ / / / / / / / / / / / / / / / / / / /

Scissors

It is wise to invest in a pair of good quality dressmaker's scissors. Not only will they last longer, but they also cut more accurately than cheaper ones. It is also important to ensure that they are comfortable to hold and handle.

A small pair of embroidery scissors or 'snips' are very useful for trimming threads.

Thimble

Thimbles are made in many sizes to fit the middle finger of the hand that holds the needle, enabling you to push the needle through the fabric with speed and efficiency, without piercing the fingertip.

Tape measure

A fibreglass tape measure is the best type to buy. Plastic or fabric tape measures may stretch over a period of time and become less accurate.

Pins

It is always best to use stainless steel pins as these will not rust. Glass-headed pins are an invaluable asset. They are easily seen and removed, and when using more open weaves, the glass head will not penetrate the fabric quite so easily. As well as the more normal uses, pins will be used for stretching the fabric prior to framing (see page 22).

Tweezers

A pair of flat-edged tweezers is a useful tool for removing loose threads if the work needs to be unpicked.

Ruler

A clear plastic 30cm (12in) ruler will be needed for blocking and charting your designs. Sometimes a metre rule is useful although not essential. A set square will help measure accurate right angles.

Tracing paper

This will be useful both for tracing shapes for designs and for creating border corners if you are making up your own designs (see pages 14–15).

Dressmaker's carbon

Dressmaker's carbon is available in white, red and blue and is used for the transferral of designs on to fabric (see page 15). This can be obtained in packs of single sheets or by the roll. I find carbon paper easiest to use, but a transfer pen or transfer pencil may also be used according to the manufacturer's instructions. If you have used any of these methods to transfer your design to the fabric, work the stitches slightly beyond the design line to avoid leaving the line showing. If marks are left on the fabric from any of these transfer methods, then careful hand washing of the finished piece in a gentle detergent will remove them. You will, however, need to stretch your fabric back into shape and allow the fabric to dry naturally (see Chapter 5).

Tailor's chalk

Tailor's chalk can be used for marking out designs and is easily removed by brushing off after use. This special chalk is usually compacted into a triangular wedge shape for ease of use and handling.

Masking tape

Masking tape is used for binding the edges of the fabric to eliminate fraying, and it prevents the threads from becoming snagged on the sides of the fabric whilst work is in progress. It can also be used for holding down the fabric when tracing off designs.

Pencils

HB and 2B pencils will be needed for tracing designs.

Sketch pad

An A4 sketch pad is usually adequate for most initial design work, although larger sheets of paper will obviously be needed for planning sizeable designs in full detail.

Graph paper

Graph paper will be necessary if you need to scale designs up or down. It may be easier for you initially than blocking the squares yourself.

Mirror

A small rectangular mirror is essential for 'cornering' designs accurately (see page 14).

Hoops and frames

The size of embroidery hoop you require will largely depend upon the overall size of the design. Ensure that you purchase a hoop large enough so that no area of the hoop is touching the design area. If it does, this will flatten the worked area and may also cause fraying. There are several types available (see Chapter 3, pages 15–17).

Ring frames or hoops These simply consist of two rings that fit inside each other with a metal adjustable screw. They come in many sizes and are widely available.

Seat frames These are round hoops with a foot-shaped base that can either sit steady on a table top or be placed between the legs and sat upon.

They generally come in 20cm (8in), 25cm (10in) and 30cm (12in) sizes.

/ /
Tip **If you are going to use one of these types of frame, it may be wise to put an old sock over the base. This will prevent any rough edges snagging on your clothes or tights.**
/ / / / / / / / / / / / / / / / / / / /

Slate frames Slate frames come in a variety of sizes and consist of rods at top, bottom and sides. The top and bottom rods have strong, coarse webbing stapled to them. This webbing is used to attach the fabric on to the rods. The side rods have adjustable screw mechanisms which tighten the fabric and keep it taut. Adjustable floor stands, available in many shapes and sizes, can be obtained for use with the slate frame

and, like the seat frame, enable the embroiderer to work with both hands.

Rotating frames These differ from slate frames in that only the top and bottom rods are fastened (usually with wing nuts) to the side frame.

Threads

There are a variety of thread types available today which can be used for crewel work, some of a more traditional nature, others offering opportunities for experimentation and different effects (see Fig 2.2).

Crewel wool

This is a fine, worsted two-ply wool which is supplied in many soft, subtle colours and is similar to one strand of Persian wool. Any number of threads can be used together, depending on

the effect you wish to achieve. It may be used for canvas work and freehand embroidery as well as crewel work. All the threads specified in this book are Appleton's crewel wool unless otherwise specified.

Persian wool

This three-stranded wool may be used complete or divided into strands. It is very good for canvas work.

Stranded cotton

Six-stranded cotton thread is available in a wide range of colours. The strands can be separated into one or two strands for finer, more delicate work. Stranded cotton can be used complete for canvas work, in two strands for cross stitch and freehand embroidery, one strand for fine detail, or as many strands together as you wish for more dense and textured effects. Two different tones of the same colour, in single strands, can be used together to give a 'tweeding' effect which blends the tones together. This is especially effective for facial details where some toning down of colour is often needed. Stranded cotton is probably the most commonly used embroidery thread.

Metallic thread

Metallic threads are now available in different weights, thicknesses, textures and styles, both real and imitation, gold, silver and 'tweeded'. The most commonly used metallic thread is Japanese gold, which consists of a thin plate of gold wrapped around a core of silk thread. Twisted gold thread is a synthetic thread of thin metallic fibres wrapped on to a thread core. Metallic threads can be used on their own for

Fig 2.2 Some of the different threads available to crewel embroiderers today: crewel wool, Persian wool, stranded cotton and metallic threads.

gold or silver work, or used to highlight or enhance areas of embroidery previously worked. They blend well with most other types of threads.

Beeswax Fine metallic threads are pulled through beeswax, which coats the thread and enables it to travel through fabric smoothly without snagging, twisting, knotting or kinking. When couching down a metallic thread (see Stitch Dictionary, page 84), the couching thread is also pulled through the beeswax to strengthen it and to help it cling to the metallic thread.

Use of threads

It is important to ensure that the threads you select for each project are those that will give you the finish and texture you desire. Using a variety of threads in differing thicknesses often creates a more interesting design and will undoubtedly enhance the overall effect.

Most of the threads and wools used in embroidery today are dye-fast and categorized as 'easy-care', but it is always wise to check the manufacturer's instructions given on the labels before you start work.

A length of yarn approximately 50cm (20in) is usually sufficient to work with. Any longer than this and you run the risk of the thread knotting, twisting or kinking. To prevent this from happening, allow the thread to hang loose and dangle from time to time during your embroidery work. Any twisting of the thread will then be eliminated.

All threads carry a label bearing a dye number or colour code. When purchasing threads or wools, ensure that you purchase sufficient quantities of the same batch to complete a project. It may not always be possible to purchase the same dye-lot or colour code later and therefore shade variations may occur. Any leftover threads or wools can always be used for other projects needing smaller quantities, so they will not be wasted.

Fabrics

Fabrics fall into three main categories: woven, knitted and non-woven.

Fabric types

Woven fabrics Woven materials consist of warp and weft threads. The warp threads run down the length and the weft threads are woven across them. The edges which turn back on

Fig 2.3 A selection of the types of fabric most suitable as backgrounds for crewel embroidery.

themselves are called selvedges.

When using a woven material, it is a good rule to have the warp threads running down and the weft threads running across to accommodate the natural stretch of the fabric. Fabrics can be woven in natural fibres such as silk, cotton, linen and wool, or synthetics such as rayon and polyester (see Fig 2.3). Closely woven, firm fabrics are ideal for crewel embroidery.

Knitted fabrics By their nature, knitted fabrics make stitching upon them difficult because of their stretching properties. You will, however, find them suitable for smocking and quilting, although they are best avoided for crewel work.

Non-woven materials Non-woven materials include felt, vinyl, leather and suede. They are generally strong, durable and hard-wearing. They do not fray when cut, have no grain and therefore can be used in any direction. Although these fabrics can be stitched, they are not generally used for crewel work.

Choosing fabric for crewel work

Most crewel work is done on linen weave fabrics. These fabrics are strong, firm and durable, but they are expensive. You may wish, therefore, to consider other possibilities such as linen and synthetic mixes, cotton or silk. The following points should be considered when selecting a fabric to avoid disappointment.

1 Is the fabric suitable for the project you wish to work?
   ❖ Will the fabric droop or sag, therefore spoiling the overall effect?
   ❖ Will the fabric need to be backed to give added strength?
   ❖ Is the fabric too fine for the weight of the thread?
   ❖ Will the fabric fray?
   ❖ Does the fabric blend with the choice of embroidery thread colours?
2 Is the fabric washable (easy-care) or will it need to be dry cleaned?
3 Will the chosen fabric be used purely as a background to the design, or will it be an integral part of the finished project?

Plain fabrics are generally best as backgrounds, although fabrics which have dots, stripes or checks can complement and enhance a design if used in a delicate manner and not allowed to dominate the overall effect. It could well be that they may even spark off a design idea. Some fabrics have a matt surface, others are shiny, some have a slub finish, others a smooth finish. Sometimes the wrong side of the fabric may seem more suitable than the right side – do not be afraid to use it if you feel it will produce a better result.

Another point to consider when buying fabric is whether or not it will shrink when washed. If you are at all concerned that the fabric may shrink on washing, take a small, measured sample piece and test it by washing it in a mild detergent. If the fabric does shrink, then the whole piece of fabric will need to be washed and pressed before using it for a project. You may need to buy slightly more fabric to allow for this.

Chapter Three

Starting Crewel Work

Crewel embroidery is worked on or above the surface of the fabric, utilizing a variety of stitches such as stem, split, long and short, satin, block shading, coral, couched and laid work, plus filling stitches such as fly, cloud, seed, buttonhole and battlement couching (see the Stitch Dictionary, pages 81–96). As these stitches are worked on or above the surface of the fabric, very little thread is wasted. Freehand embroidery stitches can also be combined with the crewel stitches.

The stitches are worked to form lines, solid and semi-solid shapes, and open fillings. Textures can be created by working the same stitch in opposite or different directions, or by using more than one strand of wool. The variations are endless, providing the embroiderer with great scope to produce a wide array of design possibilities.

Shading also plays an important role in crewel work and generally consists of rows of satin stitches or blocked shading worked in tones of one colour or graduating colour combinations to achieve the desired effect.

Making a sampler for practice

Working a small sampler is often a good way to start many forms of embroidery. This will enable you to experiment with background fabrics,

get the feel of the thread or wool, and have a practice run of the stitches you may wish to use on future projects, and assist you to co-ordinate colour. It will also enable you to judge how much stitching can be obtained from a skein of thread or wool, which in turn will help you to calculate the total number of skeins required for any further projects and the cost involved.

//////////////////////////
Tip **When stitching, avoid pulling the thread too tightly as this will thin the thread and cause uneven stitching and possibly fraying of the wool.**
//////////////////////////

Details for making a stitch sampler are given in Chapter 6, pages 29–32. There you will find patterns for leaf and flower motifs. These have been provided for you to trace off and use on your fabric for the sampler. If you do not wish to use these particular motifs, preferring to design something yourself, then you will find designing both rewarding and enjoyable. You may find inspiration from a greetings card, photograph, wallpaper or furnishing fabric. Ink blots, doodles, circles, paper cut-outs, reflections on the sea, the centre of a beautiful flower, or the grain in wood can all form the basis of a design. A design should fill the area for which it is planned in a well balanced and pleasing way. Using felt-tipped pens of different thicknesses will help you make thick

and thin lines indicating where the denser areas of embroidery should be concentrated.

Once you have settled on a design (such as Fig 3.1), you may need to enlarge or decrease it to the required size for the project you have in mind.

Enlarging and reducing designs

Grid method

There will be many sources to use for your initial design but it may not turn out to be the correct size to begin with. To scale up a design, draw a grid of about 2.5cm (1in) squares on to the original design. On to a sheet of paper large enough to accommodate the

Fig 3.1 An example of a simple design of leaves and flowers. The dotted lines indicate the correct stitch direction.

increased size of the design, mark a grid with larger squares, but make sure there are the same number of squares as you have on the first grid. Carefully copy the design outline on to the larger grid, square by square. To reduce a design, the whole procedure is simply reversed (see Fig 3.2).

Photocopy method

Draw the design outline on to a sheet of paper or trace it on to a clear acetate sheet with permanent, waterproof marker pen. You can then photocopy this to enlarge or reduce it to the exact size you require.

Cornering a border design

If you wish to enhance your design by framing it within a decorative border, the procedure to follow is not too difficult.

Draw the border design on to a sheet of paper. Place the paper on a smooth, level board or table, then take a small, flat-edged mirror (pocket size with no surround is best) and place it diagonally across the border design. The reflection of the border will appear in the mirror. You may wish to move the mirror over various areas of the design to see the different effects.

Fig 3.2 Enlarging and reducing a design using a grid.

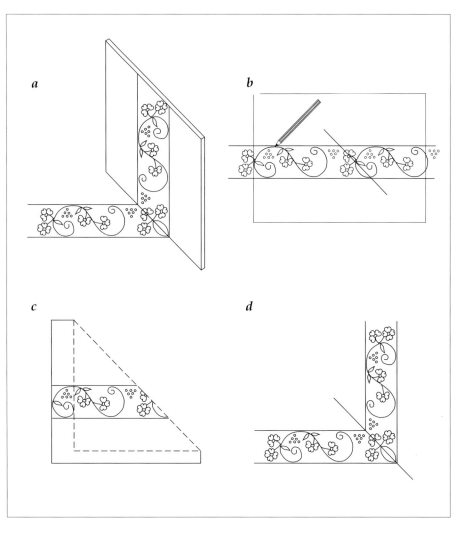

Fig 3.3 (a) Move the mirror along the border design until you are satisfied with the corner pattern. (b) Mark the corner with a diagonal pencil line and trace the border design up to the diagonal line. (c) Fold the tracing paper along the diagonal line and trace the design from the first tracing on to the top layer of folded tracing paper. (d) Open out the tracing paper to reveal a perfect corner.

When you are completely satisfied that you have made the right choice of turning point (see Fig 3.3a), hold the mirror still, take a pencil and rule a diagonal line using the straight edge of the mirror as your guide. Trace the border up to the diagonal line (see Fig 3.3b). Once you have done this, carefully fold the tracing paper over, along the diagonal line, and trace the design on to the tracing paper directly over the first tracing (see Fig 3.3c). This turned over section becomes your corner. Lift up and open out the tracing paper and then trace off the corner design alongside your original border design (see Fig 3.3d).

Transferring the design on to fabric

Once your design is complete (with or without a border), you will need to transfer it accurately on to your chosen fabric, and by far the best way to do this is to use dressmaker's carbon.

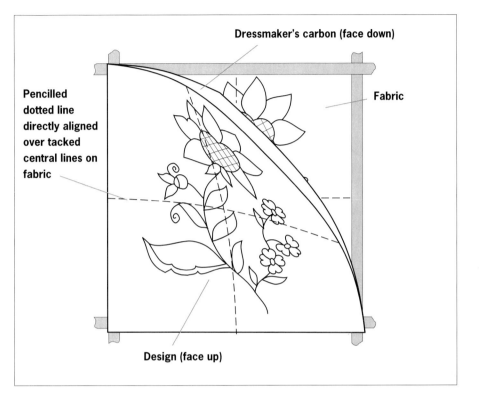

Fig 3.5 With the dressmaker's carbon face down on top of the fabric, and the design face up on top of that (dotted lines aligned with tacked lines on fabric), press firmly with a pencil to transfer the lines of the design on to the fabric.

Cover the raw edges of the fabric with masking tape first of all, to protect it from fraying or from snagging the thread during stitching. Then fold the fabric in half, press, and fold in half again the other way. Tack along the creases and smooth the fabric out (see Fig 3.4).

Now lay out the fabric on to a clean, smooth surface and fasten it down with masking tape. Fold the design in the same way as the fabric, along its central lines, then take a pencil and very lightly mark the creases with a dotted line. Smooth out the design.

Place the carbon paper face down on to the fabric, then place the design on top of this, face up. Line up the tackings on the fabric with the dotted lines on the design. Anchor the design and carbon paper down with heavy weights and trace around the outlines, bearing down quite heavily on the pencil. Lift the corner of the design and carbon paper occasionally to see how well the carbon is transferring the design on to the fabric (see Fig 3.5).

Attaching fabric to frames

When the design has been successfully transferred to the fabric, it is time to secure the fabric in a suitable frame, ready for stitching.

Choose your frame carefully, ensuring that no part of the design area is going to be flattened or squashed. A slate frame or rotary frame will be much better for larger projects.

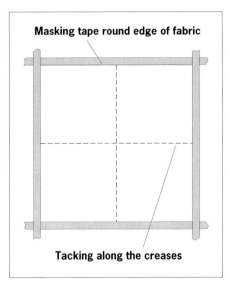

Fig 3.4 Tack along the creases in the fabric to mark the central lines.

Ring frame

To frame up a simple ring frame or hoop, place the inner ring on a flat surface. The inner ring can be bound with thin strips of cotton, cut on the bias (i.e. diagonally). This will help to protect the fabric and prevent it slipping (see Fig 3.6). Lay the fabric over the inner ring with the design uppermost. Place the outer ring over the fabric and push it firmly over the inner ring, ensuring that the fabric is taut and free of creases (see Fig 3.7). The material in the hoop should be as tight as a drum. Adjust the screw on the outer ring to secure.

Slate or rotary frame

For larger projects, a slate or rotary frame is far more practical. The width of the fabric being used must not be any wider than the webbing of the frame, but the length can be greater than that of the side poles because the

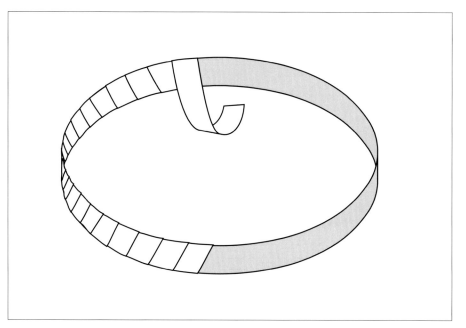

Fig 3.6 Bind the inner ring with thin strips of cotton to protect the framed fabric and hold it securely once both rings are in place.

surplus fabric may be wound around each roller. In this way, only the area to be embroidered is exposed. As the work progresses, unroll the area to be embroidered next, and roll up the finished section, enclosing a piece of tissue paper or soft material to protect the stitching.

Begin by marking the centre of the webbing with a pencil on both top and bottom rods. Measure the fabric to find the centre and mark with a pin. Line up the pencil mark with the pin and, working from the centre out, pin the fabric to the webbing. Then oversew the fabric to the webbing, without causing a ridge (see Fig 3.8). Repeat the procedure for the bottom rod. Roll up the surplus fabric. Bind the side edges of the exposed fabric with masking tape on both sides. Adjust the screws to ensure that the fabric is taut.

With strong thread, stitch through the masking tape in a criss-cross manner over the side rods as shown in Fig 3.9. This procedure will need to be repeated when more fabric is unrolled to expose the next area to be worked.

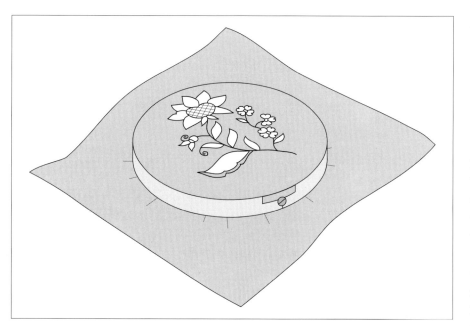

Fig 3.7 Once the outer ring is in place, pull the fabric taut between the rings and tighten the screw on the frame.

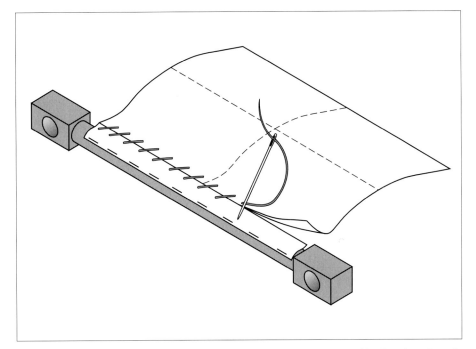

Fig 3.8 Oversew the fabric to the webbing, making sure that it is centrally placed on the rod.

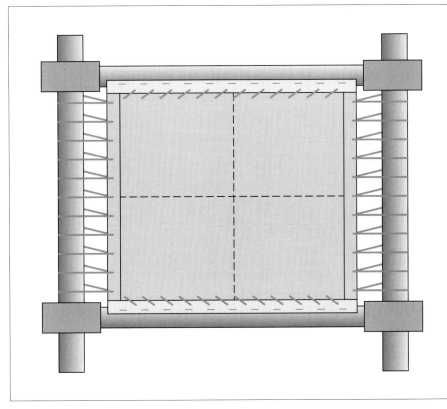

Fig 3.9 The fabric in place on the frame, with the side edges covered in masking tape and laced to the side bars.

Sometimes on the smaller frames enough tension can be achieved simply by rolling the fabric taut rather than actually lacing it to the side bars. Larger frames will, of course, always need side lacing.

Project instructions

The projects in this book have been designed for all levels, from the novice in embroidery to the more seasoned stitcher. The projects range from easy through to advanced, and there is something for everyone. Some are useful objects, others are simply ornamental and designed for visual pleasure, for yourself, your friends and your family.

Each project will give you information on the best frame to use, the overall design size, fabric dimensions, the type of fabric used and a suggested alternative, colours of thread used, along with the code numbers and the quantities involved. All code numbers refer to Appleton's crewel wool unless specified otherwise. Details of the stitches worked for each project and guidelines on stitch direction (the direction is shown by dotted lines on the patterns) are also included. Any special instructions for backgrounds and techniques for finishing off are given where appropriate.

Some of the projects are quite sizeable, so it has not always been possible to reproduce a full-size pattern for the design. In these instances it will be necessary to follow the instructions on pages 13–14 for enlarging a design, either using a grid or a photocopier.

Chapter Four

Colour and Backgrounds

Colour plays a vital role in embroidery, and however simple the project, it is always worth considering carefully the colour combinations you will use and how you wish that colour to be represented by your threads and fabric.

Experimentation with colour is an enjoyable process with few hard and fast rules. You may wish to use several tones of one colour, or have a dominant colour and other complementary colours. A basic understanding of colour will help you when you come to plan out colour schemes.

Understanding colour

Colour breaks down into three main groupings (see Fig 4.1).

1 Primary colours: pure hues of red, blue and yellow, from which, with black and white, all colours derive.
2 Secondary colours: achieved by the mixing together of two primary colours in equal quantities, e.g. red+yellow = orange; blue+yellow = green; red+blue = purple. Tertiary colours are mixtures of a primary colour and its adjoining secondary colour.
3 Achromatic colours: mixtures of black and white, i.e. greys and neutrals. When you mix together all three primary colours plus black and white (in differing proportions) the result is a range of greys and browns.

There are no hard and fast rules where colour is concerned, but a few pointers to consider for embroidery are included in the list below. You may wish to purchase shade cards. DMC, Twilleys and Appletons all offer sample cards (see Fig 4.2), or even paint shade cards would be beneficial. You may even like to create your own to see how well different colours work together.

❖ Warm colours such as reds, oranges and yellows work best if placed in the foreground or used as a focal point to a design.
❖ Red can give a sense of energy and excitement. Symbolically it is often linked with happiness and joy, and in religious symbolism it represents blood and fire.
❖ Yellow is a bright, sunny colour, representing a range of things including love, heat, wisdom and learning, spiritual enlightenment, joy and celebration.
❖ Cool colours such as blues, purples and greens lend themselves well to a feeling of depth and distance.
❖ Blue suggests calmness, serenity, spirituality, depth, sincerity, regality, and in religious symbolism, eternity, faith and truth.
❖ Green represents new growth, rebirth, fruitfulness, hope, and in religious symbolism represents the Trinity, eternal life, peace and serenity.

Fig 4.1 Colour wheel. The large wedges are the primary colours, red, blue and yellow; medium-sized wedges are the secondaries, purple, green and orange; smallest wedges are the tertiary colours. The inner ring shows the shades (formed by adding black to the basic colours), the outer ring the tints (formed by adding white).

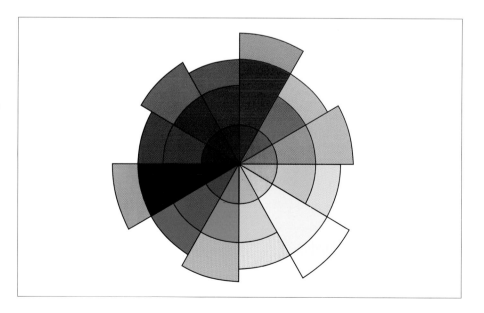

Fig 4.2 Thread shade cards from various sources, which can all help in planning successful colour combinations.

❖ Purple represents royalty, justice, knowledge, sorrow, mourning and grief.

❖ Pastel colours of all shades blend together very well, creating harmonious and delicate effects that are gentle and restful.

Texture and its effect on colour

Texture can create both subtle and startling effects in combination with colour. Using dense areas of stitching next to lighter sections of stitching in the same colour will make the denser area look darker. If the background fabric is textured, this too will appear to alter the colour of the thread. Remember also that a whole skein of thread will look darker than a single thread.

Smooth, shiny fabrics reflect the light and therefore will have the effect of lightening the thread colours, whereas matt fabrics will appear to darken the colour of the thread. This light and shade can be used to great effect in embroidery to create optical illusions. Using stitches close together and then regularly spaced can also achieve this effect (see Fig 4.3).

The denser the stitching, the bolder and more heavily textured the finished design. The more open the stitching, the more delicate and lacy the effect.

I hope that you will find experimentation with colour and stitchery as enjoyable as working a full-scale project.

Backgrounds

Once you have mastered the art of the stitches and experimented with colour, you may wish to try your hand at creating unique backgrounds for your designs rather than using readily available fabrics. This can be achieved in a variety of ways. Fabric paints, silk dyes and fabric crayons are all mediums which can be used (see Fig 4.4). If you wish to use any of these techniques, it is wise to experiment first of all on scrap fabric to find out which you feel more confident in using, and to observe the effects it will create.

Fabric paints

There are many different brands and suppliers of fabric paint, all offering a wide range of permanent, water-based colours that are non-fading, machine-washable, non-toxic, and colourfast up

Fig 4.3 (above) Texture can play an important part in the final appearance of colours in embroidery, depending on the density of the stitching.

Fig 4.4 (right) A selection of fabric paints, silk dyes and fabric crayons.

Fig 4.5 The different effects which can be achieved by applying fabric paint with a brush or sponge.

to boiling point. They can be obtained in pure colour, opaque, metallic and fluorescent. I prefer to use DEKA fabric paints, but it is, of course, a matter of personal preference. Most fabric paints can be diluted by up to 10% and this is very useful for applying 'washes' to fabric. The paints, which are intermixable, can be applied to the fabric directly from the jar or bottle, and are easy to use. They can be either brushed or sponged on to the fabric, depending on the effect you wish to achieve (see Fig 4.5).

Sponged fabric

Use a plain, white or natural-coloured, lightweight fabric such as cotton or polycotton. Synthetic fabrics have a tendency to repel the water-based paints. The fabric should **always** be washed before applying the paint, to remove the dressing that is used to

finish the fabric. If this dressing is not removed prior to painting, and the fabric is washed after it has been painted, the colour will lose its intensity and this will ruin the overall effect.

Silk or fabric dyes

There are many different types of silk dye which offer a good selection of colours that are colourfast, and either washable or dry-cleanable. They can be used on lightweight cotton or polycotton fabrics as well as silk and silk velvet. Silk dyes will flow into each other and although the fabric can be treated to prevent this from happening, that will not be necessary for the projects detailed in this book.

The dyes are applied to the fabric by brush and whilst these brushes need to be of good quality, they do not necessarily have to be made from expensive sable. I use DEKA Silk dyes which are fixed by ironing. If you are using other makes, then you will need to check the manufacturer's instructions regarding fixing.

/ /
Points to remember
- ❖ **Cotton and polycotton fabrics will need to be washed before use to ensure that the dressing is removed.**
- ❖ **The fabric will need to be stretched over a softwood frame before painting or dyeing can begin.**
- ❖ **The heavier the fabric the more absorbent it will be, therefore the more paint or dye will be used.**

/ /

Sea-salt effect

The addition of sea salt to a freshly dyed piece of fabric can result in some fascinating 'special effects' (see Fig 4.6). Mix a small amount of water with the chosen colour combinations and apply the dye to the fabric with a brush. Cover the fabric completely with the dye. Sprinkle sea salt over the fabric and leave to dry. Shake off the sea salt

Fig 4.6 Some surprising effects can be achieved by the application of sea salt to freshly dyed fabric.

and then iron to fix the dye. Once this has been completed, rinse the fabric in cold water to remove any salt residue. Allow to dry and then iron once more.

The process of painting or dyeing

Using a frame

The fabric you wish to paint or dye must be stretched on to a frame to provide a smooth, taut and flat surface upon which to work.

A frame can be constructed by using lengths of 2.5cm (1in) square softwood (softwood will enable easy entry of thumbtacks). The wood can be bought cut to size, from a local wood yard or handicraft shop. The lengths are then simply screwed or nailed together at the corners. If you are unsure about tackling this job yourself, then an old wooden picture frame is an option you may wish to consider.

Take your piece of previously laundered fabric, and cut it to the size you require, but remember to cut it slightly larger than the frame. It is advisable to have at least 5cm (2in) extra all round. This will enable you to grasp the fabric firmly when stretching it over the frame.

Place the frame on a flat surface and lay the fabric over the frame, keeping the grain of the fabric parallel to the edge of the frame. Then use thumbtacks, spaced 2.5cm (1in) apart, to pin one edge of the fabric to one side of the frame. Start from the centre and work outwards to the corners. Stretching the fabric taut, repeat the process at the opposite end of the frame. Then turn the frame around and repeat this process on the other two

sides until all the fabric is pinned (see Fig 4.7). The best results will be achieved if the fabric is stretched as tightly as possible across the frame.

Applying the paint or dye

With a brush

The paint or dye can be applied with a brush directly on to the fabric once the fabric has been stretched on a frame.

To achieve a 'wash' effect, the paint or dye can be diluted to give a more translucent look. If you are not sure how much water to use, you may wish to consider wetting the fabric itself. This can be done with a spray diffuser or with a wide paint brush. When the fabric is sufficiently dampened, paint on your colour wash with broad, even strokes.

If you are using dyes, it is at this stage that you should apply the sea salt for the mottling effect detailed on page 20, if you require.

With a sponge

Using sponges to apply paint or dye is a useful technique. Large areas can be covered quite quickly by dabbing the loaded sponge on to the fabric to produce a soft, mottled effect. Colours can be applied on top of each other until the desired result is achieved.

Spraying

Using well-diluted paint or dye in a spray diffuser is another method worth considering. If you do not wish to use a spray diffuser, it is possible to buy aerosol cans of paint or dye in a wide range of colours including pastel and metallic. Any area you do not wish to take up the paint can be covered with masking tape.

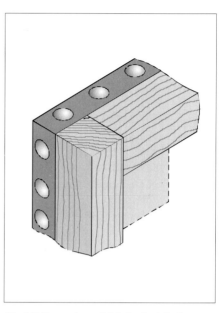

Fig 4.7 Rear view of fabric stretched tightly on a frame, pinned with thumbtacks, ready for painting or dyeing.

It must be stressed that you should use this type of aerosol spray in a well-ventilated area, away from naked flames. The sprays tend to be ozone-friendly these days, however.

Fabric crayons

Fabric crayons are applied to the fabric simply by rubbing the crayon over the fabric area. Masking tape can be applied to the fabric to cover any area you do not wish the crayons to penetrate. Fabric crayons give a 'grainy' effect. If you place the fabric on an uneven surface it is possible to obtain some very interesting and unusual results. You might like to try placing bubble-wrap or grained wallpaper underneath your fabric before rubbing on the crayon.

Most fabric crayons are generally fixed by ironing on the reverse of the fabric, but you will need to check the manufacturer's instructions.

Chapter Five

Mounting and Framing

Mounting

Mounting a piece of embroidery can make all the difference to its presentation and helps to focus attention on the work, but care is needed to choose a suitable method that will complement it well. Think carefully about how you wish the finished piece to look and the setting for which it is intended. Mounting should ideally be considered at the design stage, but this is not always possible, especially if the work being undertaken is experimental.

Preparation for mounting

The finished embroidery will need to be stretched prior to mounting. This will square it up and pull it back into shape if any distortion occurred during stitching. It is best carried out by the following method.

Place the embroidery on to a clean surface and, using a spray diffuser and cold water, dampen the embroidery all over. Cover a piece of softwood board (*at least* 5cm (2in) larger all round than your fabric) with several pieces of blotting paper or cotton sheeting. Pin out lengths of string to match the fabric dimensions (see Fig 5.1).

Dampen the blotting paper or cotton sheeting, then place the dampened embroidery on top of this inside the area marked with string. Carefully stretch and pin the embroidery out to reach the string markers, working from the centre

outwards on each side (see Fig 5.2). Allow the embroidery to dry naturally.

///////////////////////
Tip **If you are going to frame your embroidery under glass and include a window mount (coloured card surround) then the overall fabric area around the design will need to be increased to allow for this.**
///////////////////////

When the embroidery is dry, cut four strips of paper and lay them on the work while it is still on the board. Move them about until you have determined the overall mount or framing area and then pin them to the embroidery. Mark the edge of the area with pins, making a note of the dimensions. Remove the work from the board and tack along the pinned lines. Do not trim off any excess fabric at this stage.

Mounting and lacing

If the design area is small, strong card should be sufficient for mounting the embroidery. If the area is quite large, however, hardboard or 6mm (¼in) plywood may be needed. Cut the card or board slightly smaller all round than the measurements taken from the tacking lines on the embroidery. Smooth down any rough edges on the hardboard or plywood with sand paper.

Cut away any excess fabric from the embroidery, leaving at least 2.5cm

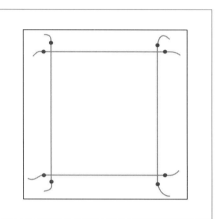

Fig 5.1 String markers pinned out on the board for stretching the embroidery.

Fig 5.2 Pin the dampened embroidery out to reach the string markers, starting in the centre of each side and working outwards.

(1in) extra all round the tacked area for a small panel, or 5cm (2in) for a larger piece. Place the embroidery right-side down on to a clean smooth surface, then place the board on top inside the tacked line. Pin the centre of each side of the fabric on to the back of the board (see Fig 5.3a).

Taking a long length of strong

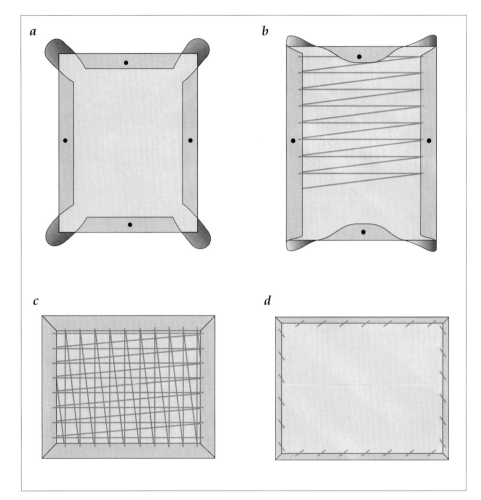

thread (a waxed cotton thread glides through the fabric smoothly), begin lacing across the board, starting from the centre and working outwards, pulling the thread tightly without bending the board. Work across the other half in the same way (see Fig 5.3b). Turn the board round and work the vertical lacing in the same way on top of the previous lacing (see Fig 5.3c).

When the lacing is finished, turn the piece over and check to ensure that there are no wrinkles or creases. Adjust if necessary.

Trim off the excess fabric at the corners neatly. You may wish to mitre the corners and instructions for this are given in Fig 5.4. Cut out a piece of backing fabric, slightly larger all round than the mount, turn the edges under and cover the laced area using small, neat slip stitches to secure (see Fig 5.3d).

Fig 5.4 (below) Mitring corners
(a) Fold each corner over at the first dotted line and crease the fabric. Trim off the excess fabric to within 6mm (¼in) of the crease.
(b) Fold over one corner and one side at a time and pin in place. Work each corner in the same way.
(c) Stitch the corners down carefully, ensuring that they do not pucker. Slip stitch down the sides.

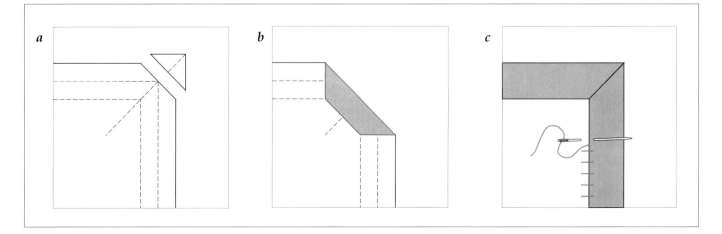

Framing

Framing can be undertaken in a variety of ways (see Fig 5.5): under glass in a picture frame, with or without a window mount, in a box frame, a fabric frame, or free-hanging from a rod.

Picture frames

Using an ordinary picture frame complemented with a window mount can be very effective. Window mounts can be cut into different shapes such as arches, ovals, circles, squares and rectangles, which can further enhance the design. Mounting card is available in a wide range of colours and weights, and can be mounted singly or with two different, complementary colours on top of one another. The wooden frame surrounds are offered in many different finishes and styles, as well as those which can be stained at home in a range of colours.

Frames and window mounts in assorted styles and sizes are readily available from good craft stores, giving you the opportunity to frame your embroidery yourself. You could, of course, take your finished piece to a local picture-framing gallery and have it professionally framed. My own local picture framers have often given me very sound and helpful advice on all aspects of framing and mounting.

Box frames

Embroidery is a tactile art form, but this has its disadvantages in that highly textured, padded, raised or beaded areas attract dust particles over time and are hard to clean

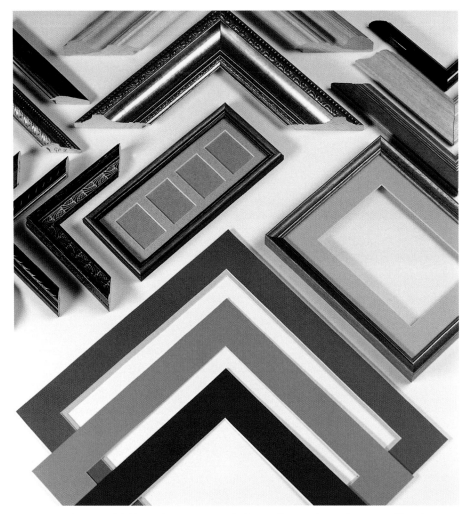

Fig 5.5 *A selection of different frame types including ordinary picture frames and box frames.*

without being damaged. Framing the embroidery in a sealed box, where small wedges of wood or compacted card are inserted around the corners and edges of the frame to lift the glass above the surface of the work, will prevent the embroidery from being squashed and also keep it completely dust free. Ready-made box frames are available, but unfortunately the choice of styles and sizes is limited. Professional framers have a good selection of box frames in all sorts of styles and weights for

this purpose and will give you helpful guidance and advice.

Fabric frames

A fabric frame is basically a window mount that is covered with a carefully selected fabric. This method of framing can enhance the overall design of the work. An aspect of the design can be echoed in stitchery on the fabric frame, or a border pattern can be created and incorporated into the fabric frame, thus becoming an integral part of the finished piece while not being allowed

Fig 5.6 (left) An aspect of the main design can be echoed by stitchery on the fabric frame.

to dominate or compete with the central design (see Fig 5.6).

The fabric can be attached to the window mount by the mounting and lacing method previously described (see page 23), or it can be glued with a suitable adhesive such as a PVA glue or Copydex craft glue (see Fig 5.7). The mount can then be attached to the edges of the embroidery by neat stitching or adhesive, or by using Velcro.

Free hanging

This method of hanging without a frame is generally used for large items such as patchwork quilts, but a smaller piece of work can look equally good if it is allowed to hang freely, suspended from a pole (see Fig 5.8).

When considering this method there are several points to remember.

Fig 5.7 (right) The method for attaching the fabric to the window mount card for a fabric frame.
(a) Place the window mount on the fabric and mark round it (both inside and outside edges), allowing half the width of the mount extra all round. Cut out the fabric, including the central window. Carefully snip the inside corners as marked.
(b) Fold over and crease the outside corners, and trim off the excess corner fabric 12mm (½in) above the crease lines. Fold the corners over again on the crease lines and press flat. Then fold over first the long edges, then the short edges, mitring the corners. Use adhesive to hold the folded fabric in place. Then fold up the edges of the inner window and glue neatly in the same way, making sure that the fabric is not puckered on the front of the frame.

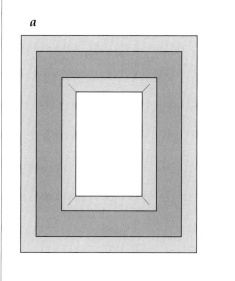

a

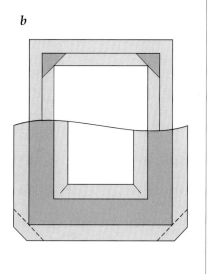

b

1 The overall fabric size will need to be increased to allow for a sleeve hem at the top of the design, and also at the bottom if the piece needs to be weighted, to accommodate the pole and weights. The top sleeve hem will need to be three times the size of the diameter of the pole. For the bottom weighted hem, this will depend on the size and type of the weights; if the weights are just pellets enclosed in a binding, for example, only a small amount of extra fabric will be needed.

2 A backing fabric will need to be attached to the embroidery prior to hanging, to give support and help prevent strain around the pole sleeve.

3 Pelmet Vilene (thicker, stiffer and heavier than normal Vilene) can be tacked on to the main fabric prior to any embroidery being worked. This will give strength to the fabric, and will help to keep the finished piece flat and even when it hangs freely. It will, however, need to be lined with backing fabric to give a neat finish to the work.

Attaching the backing

The backing fabric will need to be 4cm (1⅜in) larger all round than the finished embroidery piece. Cotton fabric is generally the most suitable.

Turn in the edges of the backing fabric and tack them down. On a

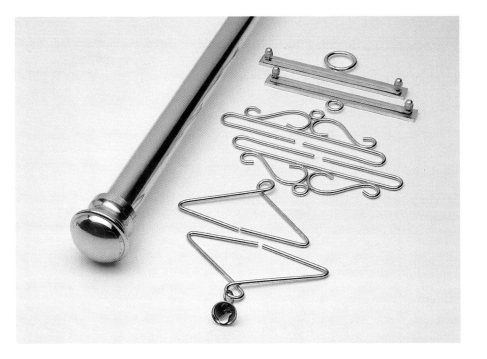

Fig 5.8 Poles and brass fittings suitable for free-hanging embroideries.

smooth, clean surface, lay the embroidered work face down and lay the backing fabric on top with the turned-in edges underneath. Smooth out any creases, keeping both fabrics flat. Tack the backing into place, then hang the fabrics on to a pole and suspend it. This will enable you to see whether the backing fabric is pulling. If it is, adjust as necessary. When you are satisfied that everything is as it should be, stitch the backing fabric to the main fabric using loose, but neat, oversewing stitches at regular intervals, ensuring that the stitches do not show through to the front of the work.

The pole should be strong enough to bear the weight of the hanging without bending. It can be wooden or brass, seen or unseen. The wooden pole can be slotted through the sleeve hem. At each end of the pole, either wooden or brass push-on knobs can be fitted to prevent the work from sliding off. A brass pole, used as a feature of the hanging, can be slotted through ornamental tabs at the top of the hanging. If the wall hanging is light in weight, it may need to be weighted down at the bottom. Weights such as those used for curtains and drapes are ideal for this purpose.

Traditional-Style Projects

Chapter Six

Stitch Sampler

MATERIALS

Finished size 23 x 23cm (9 x 9in)

Design area 18 x 21cm (7 x 8¼in)

Fabric size 28 x 28cm (11 x 11in)

Fabric type 100% mercerized cotton

Mounting board 23 x 23cm (9 x 9in)

WOOL SHADES

(1 skein of each)

Cornflower 462, 463, 464

Heraldic gold 843

Bright yellow 551

Metallic gold (Coates OPHIR 300)

STITCHES

Jacobean couching, chain, stem, buttonhole, feather, satin, split, french knots

The stitch sampler shown in the photograph has been worked from the leaf designs which you will find on page 30. The choice of leaf, flower and insect designs for the stitch sampler is yours. I have chosen just a few to enable you to see how they work together. The motifs may be linked with tendrils and feather stitches to create whatever design you wish. Experiment with the design by tracing individual leaves and flowers and moving them about on a sheet of paper. Once you have settled on a design, you can then trace the whole thing on to tracing paper and transfer it to your fabric with dressmaker's carbon, following the instructions on pages 14–15. The dimensions for this project will depend on the number of leaves and flowers you select. Sizes given below relate to the sampler shown in the photograph.

Leaf designs

Flower designs

////////////////////
Tip **If you are using a dark background fabric, then white dressmaker's carbon will be needed.**
////////////////////

Look through the Stitch Dictionary (pages 81–96) and carefully plan which stitches you will use. If you want a delicate, lacy effect, then use Jacobean couching and cloud filling stitches. For more textured areas, use satin and split stitches and french knots.

////////////////////
Tip **All shade numbers given are for Appleton's crewel wool unless otherwise stated.**
////////////////////

Method

When you have transferred the sampler design on to the fabric, place the fabric into a ring frame, pull it taut and tighten the screw. Work your chosen embroidery stitches. Remove the embroidery from the ring frame and mount and lace the finished piece by following the instructions on pages 22–4. The mounting board will need to be exactly the same dimensions as the finished size given above. Frame if required.

Insect designs

Chapter Seven

Leaf and Flower Design

MATERIALS

Finished size 18 x 23cm (7 x 9in)

Design area 16 x 18cm (6¼ x 7in)

Fabric size 28 x 33cm (11 x 13in)

Fabric type Unbleached linen furnishing fabric with 'grained' pattern

Mounting board 18 x 23cm (7 x 9in)

WOOL SHADES

(1 skein of each)

Royal blue 821, 824

Grey-green 352, 354, 356

Heraldic gold 842, 843

Autumn yellow 475

Bright rose pink 944

Biscuit brown 765, 767

Metallic gold (Coates OPHIR 300)

STITCHES

Straight, closed buttonhole, long and short, chain, satin, stem, Jacobean couching, star (double cross), french knots

ALTERNATIVE WOOL SHADES

Main flowers Coral 862, 864, 866

Leaves Drab green 331, 332, 334

French knots Terracotta 127

Flower centres Autumn yellow 473

Small flowers Coral 862

Jacobean couching Terracotta 127, Autumn yellow 473

Small straight stitches Drab green 334

This simple design is an easy piece to work, showing texture, shape and movement.

Method

Transfer the design centrally on to the fabric using the instructions given on page 15. Place the fabric into a ring frame, pull it taut and tighten the screw. Work the embroidery stitches. When the work is completed, remove it from the frame and mount and lace it following the instructions set out on pages 22–3. Strong mounting board is suitable for this piece of work.

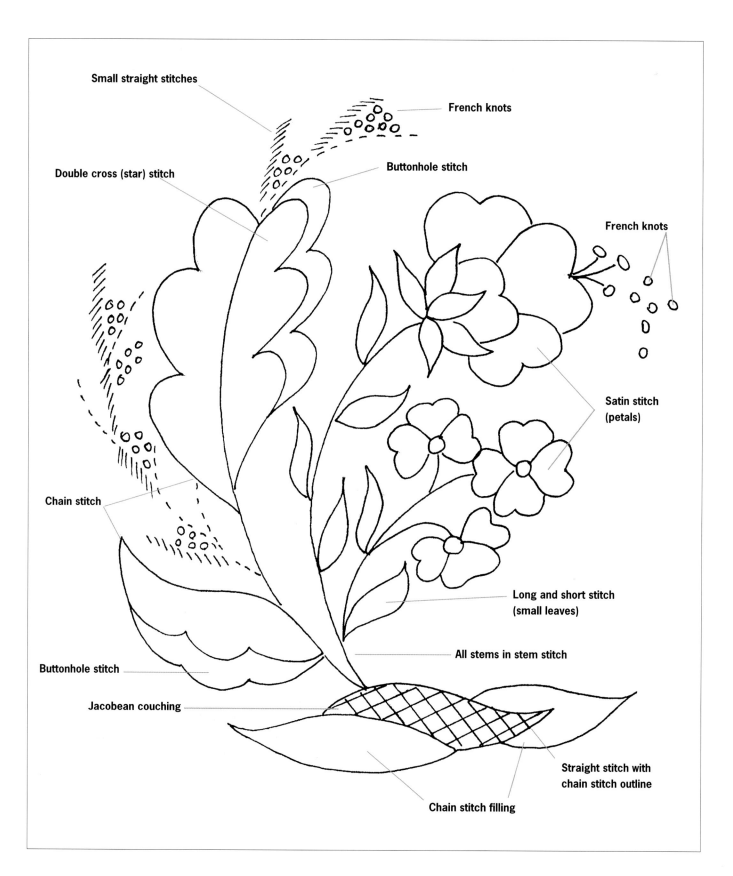

Small straight stitches

French knots

Double cross (star) stitch

Buttonhole stitch

French knots

Satin stitch
(petals)

Chain stitch

Long and short stitch
(small leaves)

All stems in stem stitch

Buttonhole stitch

Jacobean couching

Straight stitch with
chain stitch outline

Chain stitch filling

Chapter Eight

Small Panel of Flowers and Leaves

MATERIALS

Finished size 33 x 30cm (13 x 12in)

Design area 30 x 23cm (12 x 9in)

Fabric size 44 x 41cm (17½ x 16½in)

Fabric type Self-striped unbleached furnishing fabric

Mounting board 33 x 30cm (13 x 12in)

WOOL SHADES

(1 skein of each)

Early English green 541, 543, 544

Leaf green 421

Coral 862, 865

Honeysuckle 695

Bright yellow 551, 552

Biscuit brown 765

Chocolate 186

Metallic gold (Coates OPHIR 300)

STITCHES

Jacobean couching, feather, french knots, stem, chain, double cross, split, satin, straight

ALTERNATIVE WOOL SHADES

Large flower petals Wine red 711, 713, 715

Large flower centres Jacobean green 291A

Feather stitches Sea green 404

Leaves Jacobean green 291A, 294

Stems Jacobean green 292

Small flower petals Rose pink 751, 755

French knots Terracotta 124

Small flower centres Wine red 715

Jacobean couching Terracotta 121, 123, 124

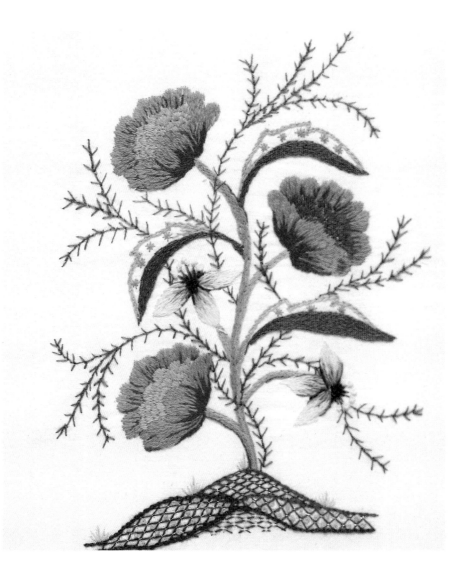

Gently bending leaves and flowers entwined with feathery fronds form the basis of this design.

Method

Cut the fabric to size. Transfer the design on to the fabric following instructions on pages 14–15, ensuring that the design is placed centrally on to the fabric.

Stitch the fabric on to a slate frame as described on pages 16–17. Work the embroidery stitches and remove the work from the slate frame.

Stretch and lace the work over the mounting board (see pages 22–3). The embroidery is now ready for framing.

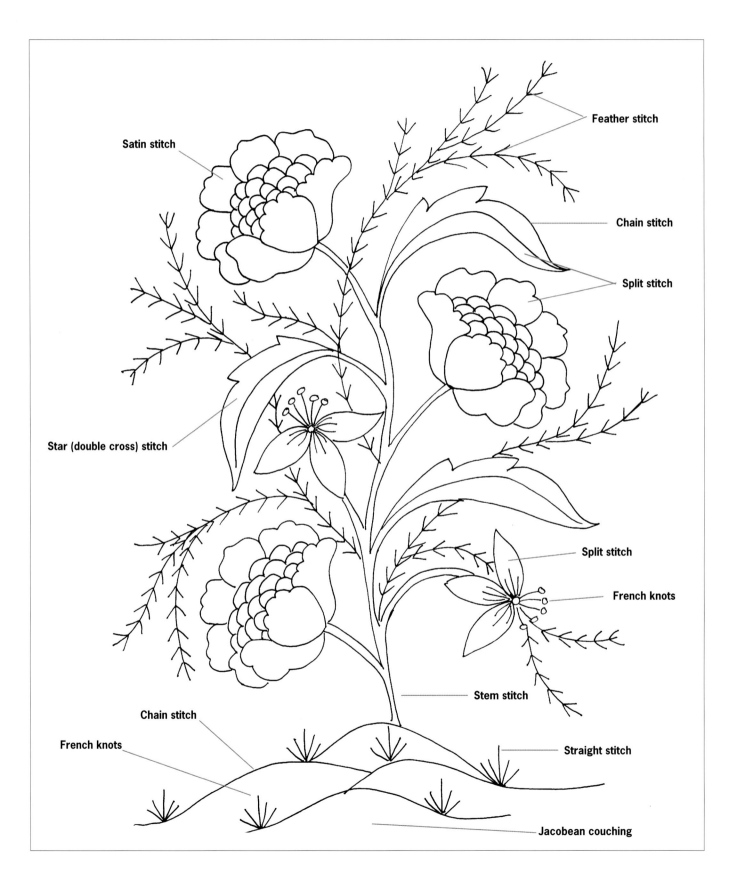

Satin stitch

Feather stitch

Chain stitch

Split stitch

Star (double cross) stitch

Split stitch

French knots

Chain stitch

French knots

Stem stitch

Straight stitch

Jacobean couching

Chapter Nine

Spectacle Case

MATERIALS

Finished size of pocket 18.5 x 9cm
(7¼ x 3½in)

Design area 15 x 7.5cm (6 x 3in)

Fabric size 42 x 24cm (16 x 9½in) (These
dimensions allow the fabric to be
placed into a ring frame)

Fabric type 100% linen with slub

Lining 40 x 13cm (16 x 5⅛in)

Dacron wadding (the 2 oz weight)
34 x 8cm (13½ x 3⅛in)

WOOL SHADES

(1 skein of each)

Kingfisher 481

Hyacinth 892, 895

Grass green 252, 254

Leaf green 422

Bright yellow 551

Black 993

Metallic gold (Coates OPHIR 300)

STITCHES

Satin, split, stem, french knots

ALTERNATIVE WOOL SHADES

Leaves Early English green 541, 543

Stems Early English green 543

Flowers Pastel shades 884, 885

Butterfly Autumn yellow 471,
Heraldic gold 841

Misplacing my spectacles is an almost everyday event for me. So that I would know where to look, I decided to make a soft case for my glasses that would fit into my embroidery workbox.

Method

With tailor's chalk mark centrally on to the fabric a rectangle of 37 x 9cm (14⅝ x 3½in) and mark the middle, i.e. 18.5cm (7¼in). Tack over the chalk marks.

Following the instructions on pages 14–15, transfer the design to the fabric, placing it centrally in the top section (i.e. the part which forms the front of the pocket on the finished case).

Place the fabric into a ring frame, pulling the fabric taut. Work the embroidery stitches and remove the completed work from the ring frame.

Cut the fabric down to 2cm (¾in) outside the tacking line all round. Fold this 2cm (¾in) allowance under and tack down, first down both sides and then along the top and bottom.

Preparing the lining

Place the Dacron wadding centrally on to the lining fabric (see Fig 9.1a). Turn the excess lining fabric over on to the wadding and tack down. Using

Stem stitch

Split stitch

French knots

Satin stitch

Split stitch

Stem stitch

small, evenly spaced cross stitches, anchor the wadding to the lining fabric (see Fig 9.1b).

Assembling the case

Find the centre point along the length of the lining and wadding and mark the spot with tailor's chalk. Mark the centre point along the length of the embroidered piece in the same way.

Place the embroidered work face down on to a clean surface, then place the lining, wadding side down, on to the embroidered piece, aligning the centre marks. Pin and tack down. With small, neat slip stitches about 3mm (⅛in) in from the edge, secure the lining to the embroidered fabric. Then fold the fabric together with the lining inside, ensuring that the corners are even. Tack down both sides to form a pocket, then oversew the side edges with small, neat stitches.

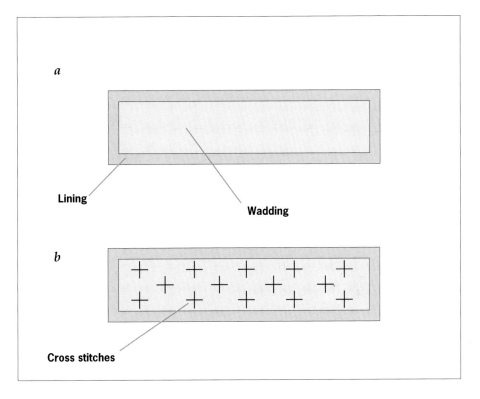

Fig. 9.1 Attaching the Dacron wadding to the lining fabric with cross stitches.

Chapter Ten

Floral Cushion Cover

MATERIALS

Finished size 41 x 41cm (16 x 16in)

Design area 36 x 35cm (14¼ x 14in)

Fabric size
Front panel: 43 x 43cm (17 x 17in)
Back panel: 2 pieces 43 x 31cm
(17 x 12in)

Fabric type Self-patterned 100%
unbleached linen furnishing fabric

WOOL SHADES

(1 skein of each)

Autumn yellow 471, 473, 475, 476, 478

Grass green 254

Leaf green 422, 427

Mid olive green 342, 344

Cornflower 463

Bright rose pink 941

STITCHES

Chain, split, satin, double cross, stem,
feather, Jacobean couching, closed
buttonhole, french knots

ALTERNATIVE WOOL SHADES

Main flowers Bright rose pink 941, 943,
944, 946

Feather stitch Sea green 404

Small flowers on leaves Bright yellow
551

Small flower centres Bright yellow 557

Leaves Grey-green 352, 353, 355

French knots Wine red 715

Leaves with Jacobean couching
Coral 862, Golden brown 901, 903,
Early English green 541

Inspiration for this design develops
from a large, star-shaped flower, with
flowers, leaves and Turkish-style leaf
motifs all radiating out from the centre.

Method

Transfer the design centrally on to the
front panel fabric, following the
instructions on pages 14–15. Stitch the

fabric on to a slate frame as described
on pages 16–17. Work the embroidery
stitches and remove the fabric from the
frame.

Assembling the cushion

Prepare the pieces for the back of the
cushion. On each piece, fold under one
end of the fabric by 2cm (¾in) and hem,

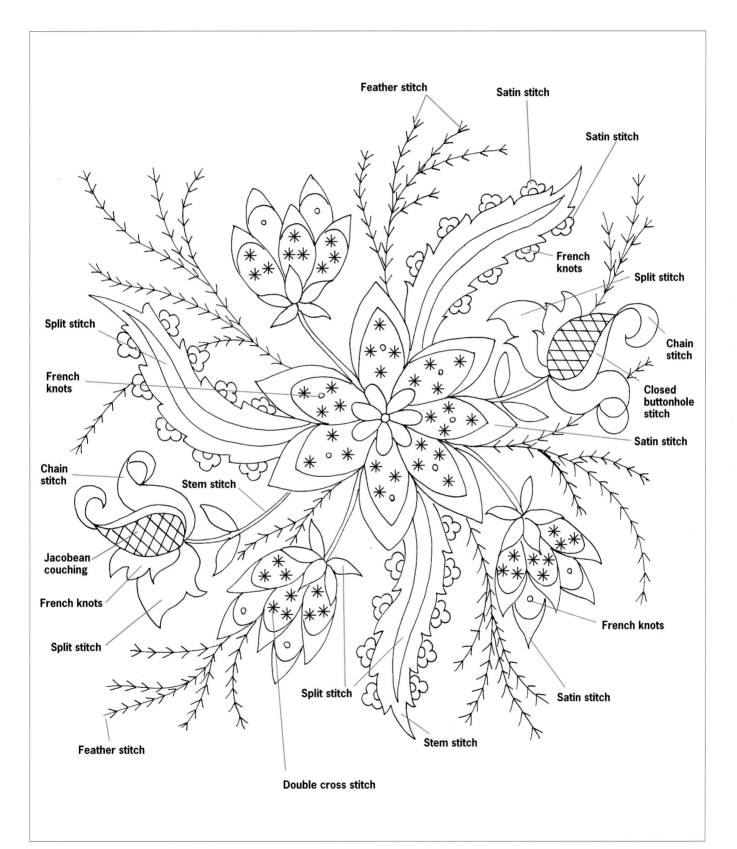

Feather stitch

Satin stitch

Satin stitch

French knots

Split stitch

Split stitch

Chain stitch

French knots

Closed buttonhole stitch

Satin stitch

Chain stitch

Stem stitch

Jacobean couching

French knots

French knots

Split stitch

Split stitch

Satin stitch

Feather stitch

Stem stitch

Double cross stitch

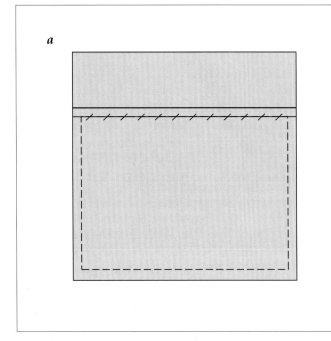

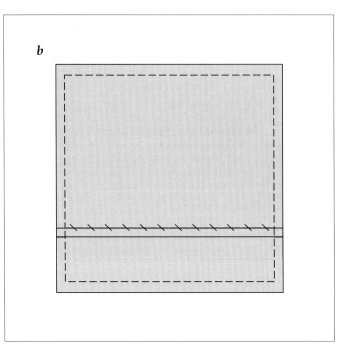

Fig 10.1 Assembling the cushion.

or machine stitch if you prefer.

Place the front panel, with the design uppermost, on to a clean, flat surface. Position one piece of the back cover fabric (wrong side uppermost) on top of the front panel, matching the bottom corners and edges and with the hemmed edge towards the centre. Tack in place (see Fig 10.1a).

Place the other back cover (wrong side uppermost) on to the top edge of the front panel, overlapping the first piece, again with the hemmed edge towards the centre (see Fig 10.1b). Tack in place.

Machine or back stitch along the tacking line 1.5cm (⅝in) from the fabric's edge. Reinforce at the side edges where the flaps meet with several extra stitches. Trim the excess fabric carefully from the four corners to reduce bulk. Turn the cushion right side out and insert the cushion filling between the flaps.

Chapter Eleven

Bell Pull

MATERIALS

Finished size (excluding brass fittings)
15 x 85cm (6 x 33½in)

Design area 15 x 77cm (6 x 30½in)

Fabric size 21 x 101cm (8¼ x 40in)

Fabric backing 100% cotton 21 x 101
cm (8¼ x 40in)

Fabric lining 100% cotton 21 x 101cm
(8¼ x 40in)

Fabric type 60% wool, 40% cotton

Alternative fabric suggestion 100%
linen slub

WOOL SHADES

(1 skein of each)

Orange red 441, 443, 444

Scarlet 504

Grey-green 352, 353, 354, 355

Olive green 242

Brown olive 311, 312, 315

Autumn yellow 471, 473, 475, 478

Terracotta 127

STITCHES

Straight, satin, stem, split, french
knots

ALTERNATIVE SHADES

(for poppies only)

Bright mauve 451, 453, 454, 456

Bright rose pink 941, 943, 945, 947

Flamingo 621, 622, 623, 626

Bright yellow 551, 553, 555, 557

Method

Transfer the design centrally on to the
fabric, following the instructions on
pages 14–15. If you are using a
wool/cotton mix fabric, you will need
to press down quite firmly to transfer
the design. You may need to go round
the design with a soft pencil after you
have used the dressmaker's carbon, to
make the details a little clearer.

Cut out the backing fabric and tack
it to the wrong side of the main fabric,
ensuring that it is flat and unwrinkled.
Stitch both fabrics on to a slate frame as
described on pages 16–17.

Start the embroidery at the top end
of the design. This will enable you to
roll the fabric on to the top rod of the
frame as work progresses.

When the embroidery has been
completed, remove the work from the
slate frame and mark the centre point
at the top edge of the main fabric.
Measure 7.5cm (3in) on either side of
the centre point (15cm (6in) in total),
and mark both places. Mark the same
points at the bottom of the fabric. Find
the threads nearest to these marks at
the top and bottom, and gently pull
these threads out along the whole
length of the main fabric. This will give
you a guide for turnings and will help
ensure that the fabric is the correct
width along the whole length of the
finished bell pull.

Turn the embroidered fabric and its
backing carefully under at the sides,
along the lines made by the threads you
removed. Pin and tack the turns in place.

Take the top brass fitting and fold the fabric over the bar to form a sleeve. Tack the sleeve hem in place, ensuring that the hem is level. Repeat the process for the bottom brass fitting.

Cut out the lining fabric, turn the edges under and tack. Pin the lining fabric to the back of the embroidery, first laying the main fabric face down on a clean, flat surface. Start at the top and work down one side, smoothing the fabrics as you proceed. Repeat this down the other side. Now tack the sides and remove the pins. Turn over the hem allowance and tack the top edge only.

Lift the work by the brass poles and hang it up from the top to see if the fabrics are pulling or puckering anywhere. If they are, then ease the tackings from the top edge along the length of the bell pull. When you are satisfied that the work is hanging properly, turn over the bottom hem and tack this also.

Now secure both sides with small neat slip stitches, working from the top edge along the length. Finish the top edge and then the bottom edge in the same way.

Gently press the fabrics, ensuring that the embroidery is not flattened, then hang the bell pull up again to allow the fabrics to settle.

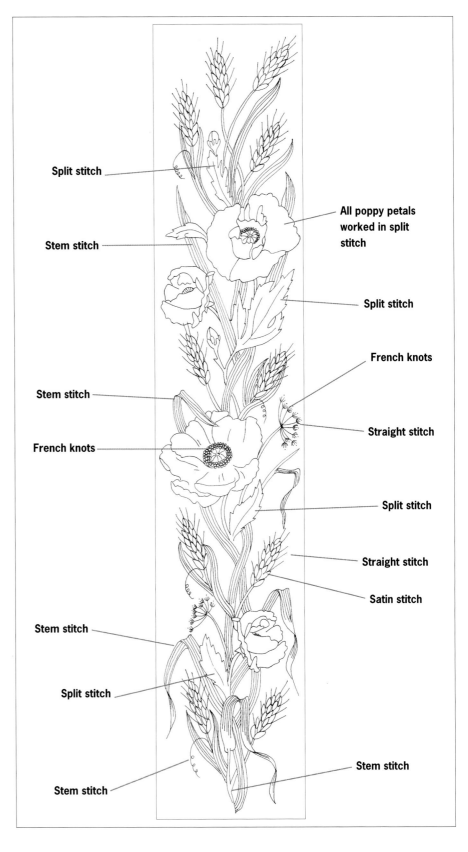

Split stitch

All poppy petals worked in split stitch

Stem stitch

Split stitch

French knots

Stem stitch

Straight stitch

French knots

Split stitch

Straight stitch

Satin stitch

Stem stitch

Split stitch

Stem stitch

Stem stitch

Exotic Birds and Butterflies

MATERIALS

Finished size 56 x 45cm (22 x 17¾in)

Design area 52 x 42cm (20 x 16⅝in)

Fabric size 66 x 55cm (26 x 22in)

Fabric type 100% cream cotton

Mounting board 6mm (¼in) plywood
56 x 45cm (22 x 17¾in)

WOOL SHADES

(1 skein of each)

Leaf green 421, 423, 424, 425, 428

Pastel shades 872, 874

White 991B

Black 993

Bright rose pink 941, 942, 944

Grass green 251A

Royal blue 821, 822, 824

Autumn yellow 471, 473, 474, 475

Bright yellow 551, 553

Coral 861, 862

Biscuit brown 761, 764, 766

STITCHES

Satin, split, straight, detached chain,
back, feather, stem, french knots

ALTERNATIVE WOOL SHADES

Birds Orange red 441, 444, 447
Scarlet 503, 505

Flowers Autumn yellow 471, 473, 475

Flower centres Autumn yellow 478

Branches Red fawn 301, 303, 305

Leaves Turquoise 523, 525, 526

Butterflies Pastel shades 871
Custard yellow 851
Replace white with Heraldic gold 841

Oriental-style birds in brilliant colours perch on the boughs of a flowering cherry tree to form the focal point of this colourful design.

Method

Transfer the design centrally on to the fabric following the instructions on pages 14–15. Then stitch the fabric on to a slate frame as described on pages 16–17.

Start the embroidery work at the top of the fabric, rolling the fabric over the top rod of the frame as work progresses. Remove the work from the slate frame when completed.

Stretch and lace the work over the 6mm (¼in) plywood as described on pages 22–3. The work is now ready for framing.

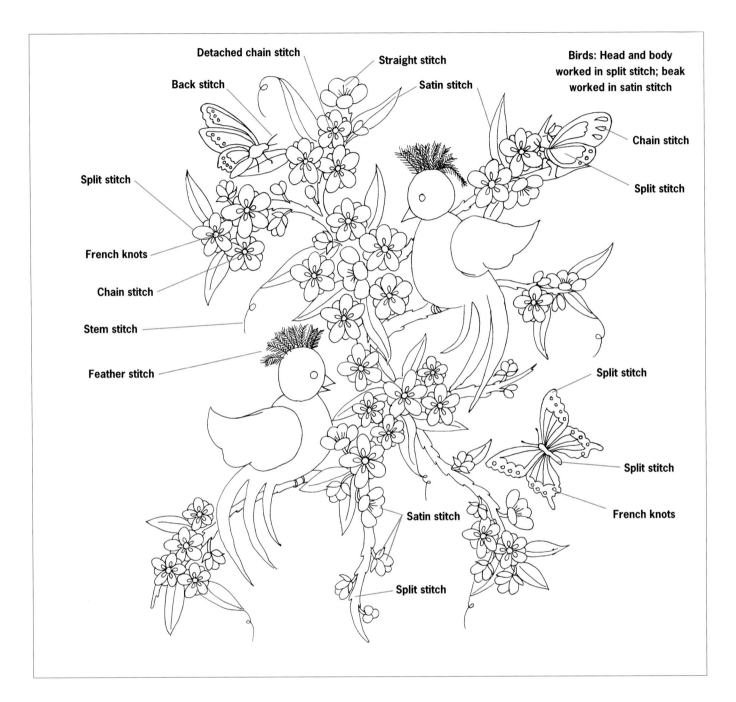

Detached chain stitch

Straight stitch

Back stitch

Satin stitch

Birds: Head and body
worked in split stitch; beak
worked in satin stitch

Chain stitch

Split stitch

Split stitch

French knots

Chain stitch

Stem stitch

Feather stitch

Split stitch

Split stitch

French knots

Satin stitch

Split stitch

/ / / / / / / / / / / / / / / / / / / /

Tip If you wish to use a colour-
toning surround mount with the frame,
you will need to increase the amount
of fabric by 5cm (2in) all round. The
size of the plywood will also need to
be increased by the same amount.

/ / / / / / / / / / / / / / / / / / / /

Chapter Thirteen

Writing Pad Case

MATERIALS

Finished size 23 x 23cm (9 x 9in) (opens like a book)

Design area The area needed will depend on the letters chosen

Fabric size (outer covers x 2) 28 x 28cm (11 x 11in)

Inner linings 23 x 23cm (9 x 9in) with pockets of 23 x 9cm (9 x 3½in); allow 3cm (1⅛in) all round for turnings

Binding (cut from main fabric) 23 x 5cm (9 x 2in); allow 3cm (1⅛in) all round for turnings

Fabric type Zweigart 3281 Cashel Linen (28 count), Colour 511 (outer covers); Silk dupion (inner linings and pockets)

Piping braid (optional) 2m (2¼yd)

Plywood or mounting board 2 pieces, 23 x 23cm (9 x 9in)

////////////////////////

Tip **If using 100% wool fabric, a backing fabric the same size will need to be tacked on to the cover fabric. This will give added strength when stretching and lacing the finished pieces.**

////////////////////////

WOOL SHADES

(1 skein of each)

Royal blue 821

Autumn yellow 471, 473

Brown olive 313

Signal green 434

STITCHES

Chain, detached chain, stem, split, satin, french knots

ALTERNATIVE WOOL SHADES

Letters Bright mauve 453

Flowers Cornflower blue 462, 463

French knots Bright yellow 552

Leaves Leaf green 423

This illuminated writing pad case was designed and worked for the birthday of a family member, and bears her initials. The whole alphabet is included here, illuminated in the style of Celtic lettering for your use. Any letters that you choose may be linked together.

47

Method

Trace the letters you require from the alphabet on pages 49–51 on to tracing paper. Then on a sheet of drawing paper work out the position of the individual letters in a pleasing design. Take another piece of tracing paper and trace off your arrangement. Transfer the design on to one of the pieces of fabric for the front cover, following the instructions described on pages 14–15.

////////////////////////

Tip **White or yellow dressmaker's carbon is best suited for dark fabrics.**

////////////////////////

Place the fabric into a ring frame and work the embroidery. When complete, follow the instructions for mounting and lacing on pages 22–3 to stretch and lace the worked piece on to the plywood or mounting board. Stretch and lace the plain outer back cover in the same way.

Stitch the piping braid all round the outer edges of both covers, neaten the joins and secure on the inside edge. To make the central binding, fold the fabric piece lengthwise with right sides together. Stitch down the long side edge and one narrow edge with back stitches. Clip the corners of the stitched-up narrow edge to reduce the bulk. Turn right side out by inserting

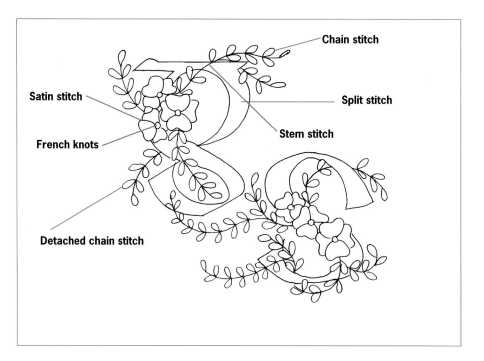

the blunt end of a pencil into the tube and working the fabric up the length of the pencil until the fabric is turned out. Fold the unstitched edge inside and oversew neatly. Stitch the binding to the inside edges of the covers to form a book (see Fig 13.1).

Cut two pieces of lining fabric 26 x 26cm (10 x 10in) and two pieces 26 x 12cm (10 x 4¾in) to form the pockets. On each pocket piece turn under and hem one of the long sides. Place one pocket on to each lining fabric piece as indicated in Fig 13.2 and tack in position.

Turn under 1.5cm (⅝in) all round

the inner linings and tack. Carefully pin the linings over the laced sections on the board, face up and with the corners matching. With a strong thread, stitch through the linings into the fabric turnings of the laced boards, with small, neat oversewing stitches. The pockets are now ready to hold notepaper and envelopes.

Fig 13.1 (below left) The binding strip sewn to the inside edges of the front and back covers.

Fig. 13.2 (below) The inside pocket in place on a lining piece.

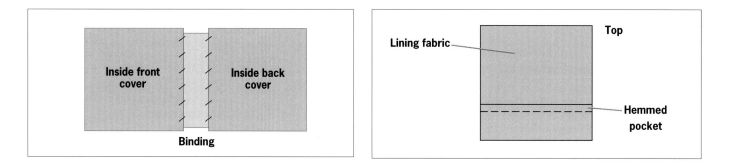

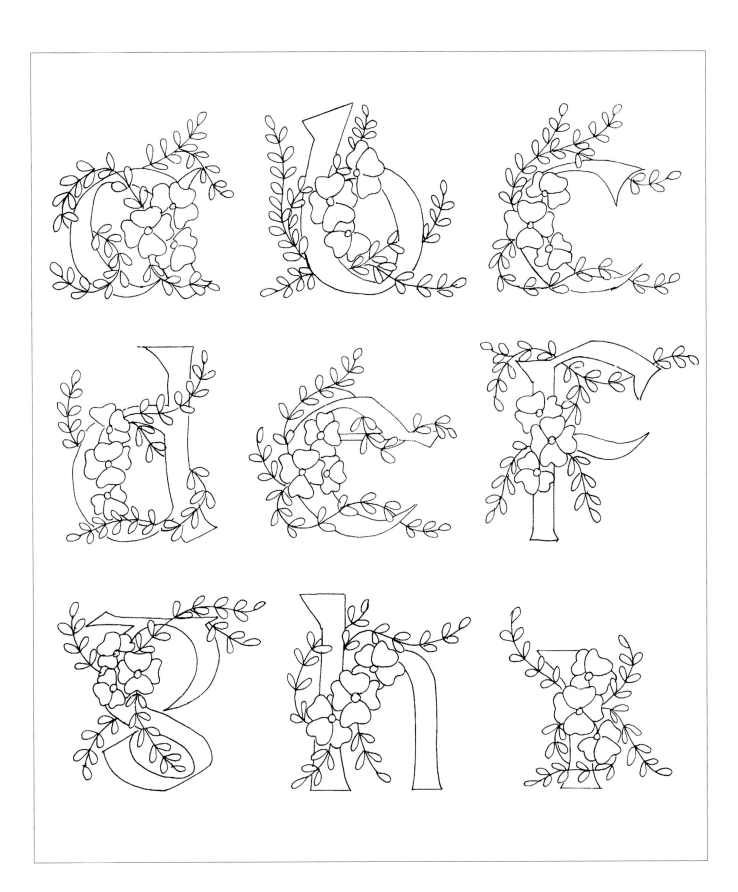

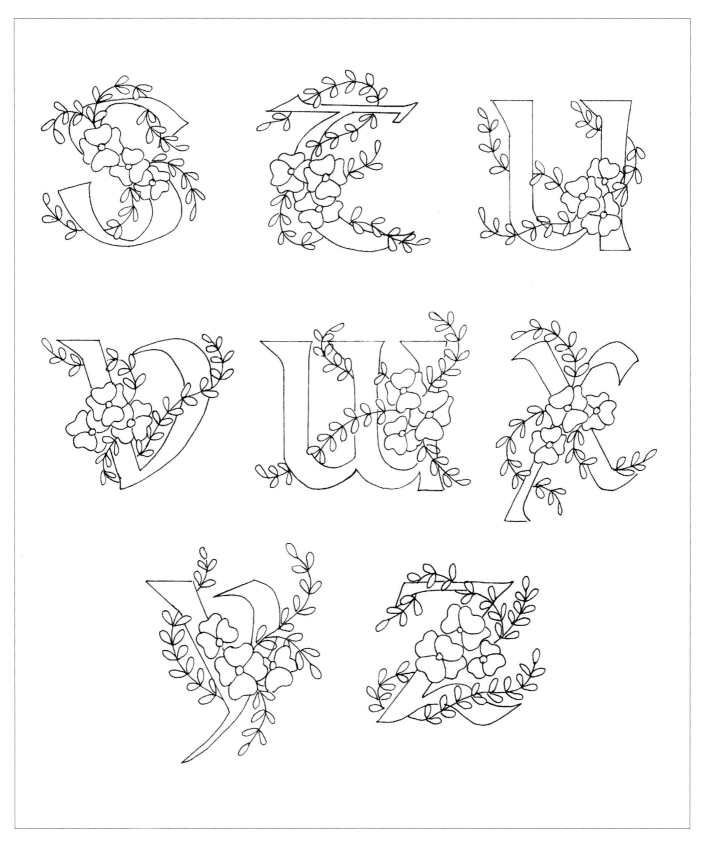

Chapter Fourteen

Jacobean Firescreen

MATERIALS

Finished size 41 x 51cm (16 x 20in)

Design area 29 x 40cm (11½ x 15¾in)

Fabric size 46 x 56cm (18 x 22in)

Fabric type Self-striped, unbleached linen furnishing fabric

Plywood or mounting board 6mm (¼in) thick, 41 x 51cm (16 x 20in)

WOOL SHADES

(1 skein of each)

Autumn yellow 471, 473, 475, 478

Honeysuckle yellow 693, 698

Heraldic gold 841

Golden brown 901, 905

Coral 862

Early English green 541, 543, 544, 547

Elephant grey 974

STITCHES

Chain, stem, split, buttonhole, closed buttonhole, satin, feather, cloud filling, french knots, Jacobean couching

ALTERNATIVE WOOL SHADES

This particular piece was designed with autumnal colours in mind, but alternative shades could incorporate Wine red, Bright rose pink, Bright mauve with small hints of Cream and Pale yellow, or Kingfisher, Sea green, Turquoise and Bright peacock with hints of Heraldic gold and Flamingo. Bear in mind the decor of the room.

The glorious array of autumnal colours, and strong winds bending the branches of trees, gave me the inspiration for this project.

Method

Transfer the design on to the fabric centrally, following the instructions set out on pages 14–15. Mark the centre points at the top and bottom of the fabric in preparation for attaching to a slate frame, then attach it to the frame as described on pages 16–17.

Start the embroidery work at the top of the fabric, rolling it on to the top rod as the work progresses. When the embroidery is completed, remove the work from the frame and mount and stretch it on to board according to the directions given on pages 22–3.

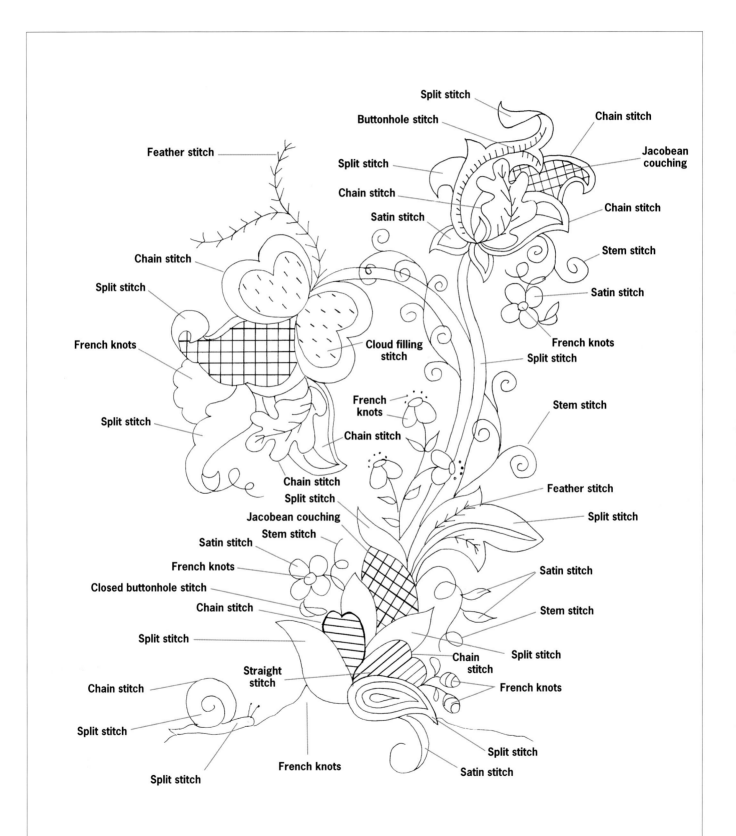

Split stitch

Buttonhole stitch

Chain stitch

Feather stitch

Split stitch

Jacobean couching

Split stitch

Chain stitch

Chain stitch

Satin stitch

Chain stitch

Stem stitch

Split stitch

Satin stitch

French knots

Cloud filling stitch

French knots

Split stitch

French knots

Split stitch

Stem stitch

Chain stitch

Chain stitch

Feather stitch

Split stitch

Split stitch

Jacobean couching

Satin stitch

Stem stitch

French knots

Satin stitch

Closed buttonhole stitch

Stem stitch

Chain stitch

Split stitch

Satin stitch

Split stitch

Chain stitch

Straight stitch

Chain stitch

Chain stitch

French knots

Split stitch

Split stitch

Split stitch

French knots

Satin stitch

Chapter Fifteen

Tulip Design

MATERIALS

Finished size 26 x 26cm (10 x 10in)

Design area 23 x 23cm (9 x 9in)

Fabric size 38 x 38cm (15 x 15in)

Fabric type 100% Irish linen

Mounting board 26 x 26cm (10 x 10in)

WOOL SHADES

(1 skein of each)

Coral 861, 862, 864

Heraldic gold 841

Autumn yellow 472, 473, 474

Kingfisher 481, 484

Grey-green 353, 354

Metallic gold (Coates OPHIR 300)

STITCHES

Split, satin, chain, spider's web, closed
buttonhole, french knots, back

ALTERNATIVE WOOL SHADES

Large tulip petals Hyacinth 891, 892,
892, 894 (mixed)

Flowers inside petals Custard yellow
851

Flower centres Turquoise 525

Small tulip petals White 991, 991B, 992
with varying shades of Turquoise
521, 524, 525

Petals highlighted with Metallic silver

Delicate coral, gold and yellow shades, highlighted in metallic gold thread, bring out the delicacy of this Turkish-style tulip design.

Method

Transfer the design centrally on to the fabric following the instructions on pages 14–15.

Place the fabric in a ring frame and work the embroidery. Remove the work from the frame when completed and stretch and lace it as described on pages 16–17. A circular surround or window mount would enhance this design.

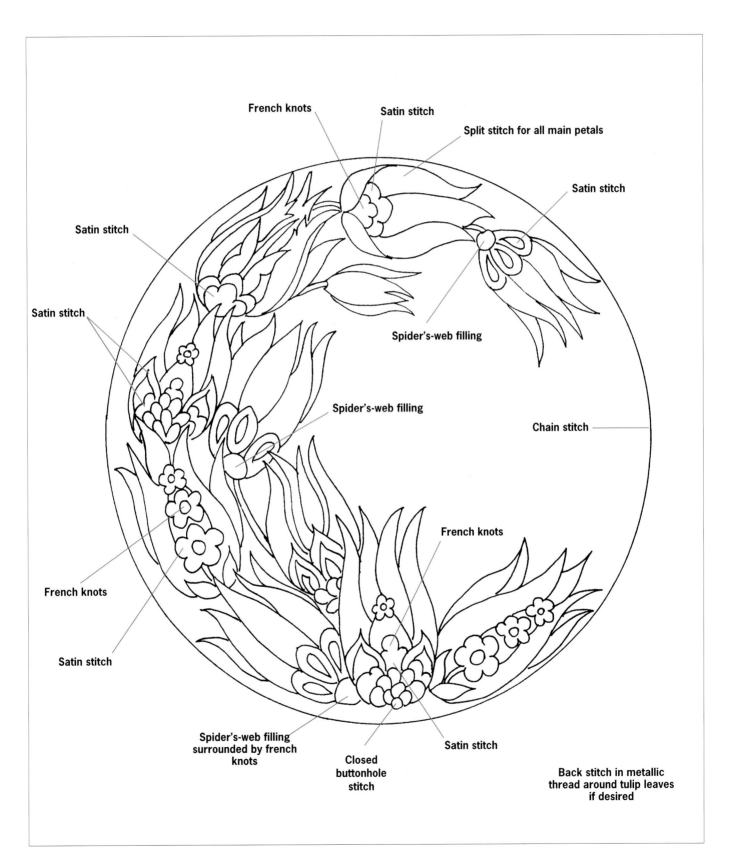

French knots

Satin stitch

Split stitch for all main petals

Satin stitch

Satin stitch

Satin stitch

Spider's-web filling

Spider's-web filling

Chain stitch

French knots

French knots

Satin stitch

Spider's-web filling
surrounded by french
knots

Closed
buttonhole
stitch

Satin stitch

Back stitch in metallic
thread around tulip leaves
if desired

Modern-Style Projects

Chapter Sixteen

Butterfly Box

MATERIALS

Finished size 22 x 22 x 8cm (8¾ x 8¾ x 3¼in)

Fabric size 1m (1yd) of 114.5cm (45in) wide fabric needed in total

Fabric type Strong cotton or furnishing fabric

Plywood (6mm (¼in) thick) or strong mounting board 22 x 78cm (8¾ x 30½in)

White cotton piping cord (to be space dyed) 1.5m (1½yd)

Braiding (only if using plywood) 1.8m (2yd) of 13mm (½in) thick braid

Silk dyes 3 or 4 to match wool shades

1 skein stranded cotton embroidery thread (to match any dye chosen)

WOOL SHADES

(1 skein of each)

Leaf green 422

Cornflower 461, 463, 464, 465

Bright rose pink 941, 945

Bright yellow 551

Black 993 (short length only)

STITCHES

Straight, detached chain, split, satin, french knots

ALTERNATIVE WOOL SHADES

Main body Bright peacock blue 831, 833

Edges of wings Turquoise 522, 525

Main inner section of wings Flamingo 622, 624

Circles and misshapes Flesh tints 702, Red fawn 300

Chain-stitch flowers Flamingo 623

French knots Turquoise 525

Straight-stitch trellis Turquoise 522

Butterflies are really fascinating creatures and make wonderful subjects for embroidery designs. All the different wing patterns provide a myriad of colours and shapes for inspiration. You could use the box to store your threads or trinkets, or perhaps it would make an appropriate gift for someone special.

Method

First cut out all the fabric pieces for the outside, as shown in Fig 16.1. Then cut out the plywood or mounting board, following the dimensions shown in Fig 16.2. On one of the 25cm square (10in square) pieces of fabric, transfer the design centrally, following the

instructions on pages 14–15.

Place the fabric in a ring frame and work the embroidery. Remove the work from the frame, then stretch and lace it over one of the square pieces of plywood or mounting board, as described on pages 22–3. Stretch and lace the unworked fabric square over the other square piece of board.

On the long length of fabric mark out the four side sections with tailor's chalk, leaving at least 5cm (2in) between and around each of the sides. This extra fabric will be needed for stretching and lacing the side sections. **Do not** cut the separate sections out yet. Transfer the side design on to each marked-out section

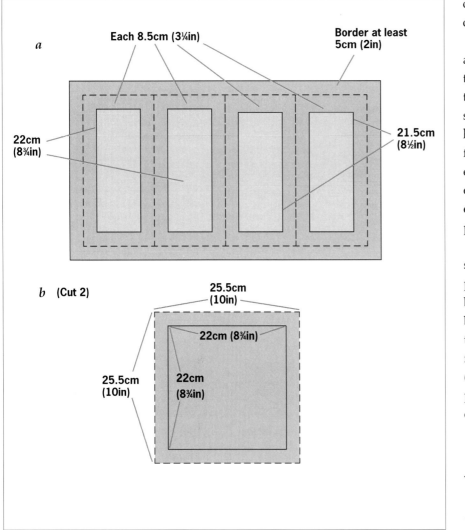

a

Each 8.5cm (3¼in)

Border at least
5cm (2in)

22cm
(8¾in)

21.5cm
(8½in)

b (Cut 2)

25.5cm
(10in)

22cm (8¾in)

25.5cm
(10in)

22cm
(8¾in)

on the fabric. Cut out the whole piece of fabric.

Place the fabric into a ring frame and work the first side section. When this section has been completed, move the fabric in the frame on to the next section and so on until all four sides have been completed. Remove the fabric from the ring frame and cut each section out. Remember to leave enough fabric around the edges of each one for stretching and lacing purposes.

Stretch and lace these four sections on to the appropriately sized pieces of plywood or mounting board. If you are using mounting board, oversew the section lengths together in the following order to form a strip: 22 + 21.5 + 22 + 21.5cm (8¾ + 8½ + 8¾ + 8½in). If you are using plywood, stitch the braid along the outside (right side) edges as indicated

Fig 16.1 (left) The dimensions for all the fabric pieces.

Fig 16.2 (below) a The dimensions for the plywood or mounting board pieces. (b) Order of assembly.

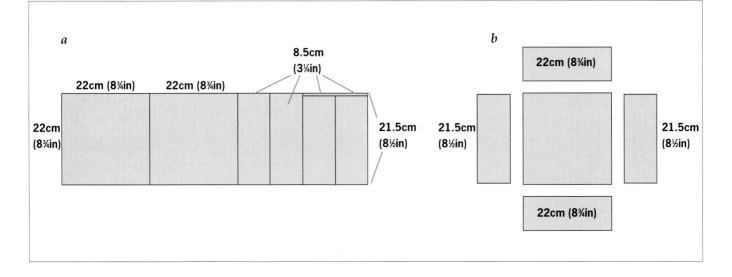

a

22cm (8¾in)   22cm (8¾in)

8.5cm
(3¼in)

22cm
(8¾in)

21.5cm
(8½in)

b

22cm (8¾in)

21.5cm
(8½in)

21.5cm
(8½in)

22cm (8¾in)

Isolated (detached) chain stitch

French knots

Straight stitch

**Butterfly body (apart from circles)
is worked entirely in split stitch**

French knots

Circles worked in satin stitch

Butterfly box pattern

Fig 16.3 (below) The positions for the braid pieces if using plywood.

in Fig 16.3. Cut the braid slightly larger top and bottom and then turn over a neat, flat hem to give the braid a tidy finish. The hemmed edge will be on the inside of the box.

Now cut four pieces of fabric measuring 25 x 11.5cm (9¾ x 4¼in). Turn under 1.5cm (2in) all round each

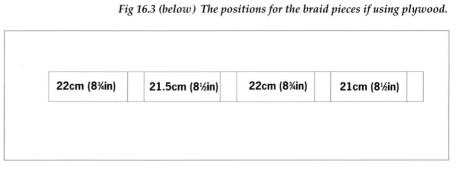

	22cm (8¾in)	21.5cm (8½in)	22cm (8¾in)	21cm (8½in)	

of the four pieces of fabric and tack. Carefully pin each piece to the fabric area of the laced face of the side sections and secure with small, neat stitches. Stitch the first side panel to the last side panel to form a square.

Now cut two more 25cm (10in) square pieces of fabric, turn under 1.5cm (⅝in) all round each piece and tack. Place one of the squares on the laced side of the box lid, matching the corners and sides, and pin in place. Stitch the lining neatly to the fabric turnings of the laced area. Repeat this process for the lining on the base of the box.

If you have been using mounting board, stitch the sides with neat oversewing stitches to the base of the box. To help keep the side pieces from moving away from the base whilst stitching, stretch elastic bands in a criss-cross fashion over the base and sides. You will, of course, have to bring the thread under the elastic bands as

the stitching progresses.

If you have been using plywood, attach a continuous length of braid (the length should fit round the four sides, plus a little extra to join together) all round the base of the box with neat oversewing stitches. Place the sides of the box on the base, inside the braid, secure the braid to the sides with pins, then oversew all round the sides to secure.

Stitch a piece of braid along the length of the outer edge (right side) of the lid to make the hinge, tucking a small section of the braid underneath to neaten the edges. Attach the other edge of the braid to the corresponding side of the box.

Now soak the piping cord in cold water and squeeze out the excess. Spread a sheet of polythene on to a flat surface and lay the cord out along the polythene sheet. Using three or four silk dye colours of your choice (to match the wool shades used), paint sections of

colour along the whole length of the cord. Allow to dry thoroughly.

Mark the centre point on the front edge of the lid with a pin. Leaving a piece of cord at least 10cm (4in) long hanging down from the centre pin, attach the space dyed cord to the fabric all round the edge of the lid with small neat stitches, until the centre pin is reached once again. Allow another 10cm (4in) of cord to hang down alongside the previous length. Take a length of embroidery thread matching one of the colours of the dyes used, and stitch into the two pieces of hanging cord as near to the lid edge as possible. Wrap the thread around the cord neatly and quite tightly until a 'neck' is formed, then stitch through the cord several times to secure. The top of the tassel is formed in this way. Unravel the loose cording completely to form the tassel skirt and trim off any uneven ends at the bottom.

Chapter Seventeen

Needlework Organizer

MATERIALS

Finished size 45 x 20cm (17¾ x 8in)

Front design area 18 x 14cm (7 x 5½in)

Main fabric size 60 x 50cm (23⅝ x 19⅝in)

Fabric type 100% white cotton quilting

Inner fabric size 45 x 45cm (17¾ x 17¾in)

Fabric type 100% white cotton

DEKA Silk dyes Purple and carmine

Sea salt

Narrow ribbon 2m (6ft 6in)

Soft white or cream fabric 25.5cm (10in) square

WOOL SHADES

(1 skein of each)

Bright mauve 451, 455

Bright rose pink 943

Metallic gold (Coates OPHIR 300)

STITCHES

Straight, detached chain, cross, split, french knots, interlaced running, Jacobean couching, herringbone

ALTERNATIVE DYES AND WOOL

The colour alternatives for the embroidery will depend on the colours chosen for dyeing the fabric. Alternative green and blue shades are given here, but you may wish to use a selection of pastel shades (add white mixer to the dyes) and use lighter and darker shades of wool to highlight the embroidery.

Dyes Turquoise, Grun

Wools Kingfisher 481, 484, Signal green 431, Metallic silver (Coates OPHIR 301)

Patchwork diamond and baby blocks worked together to form a pattern were the inspiration for this particular project. I used specially dyed fabrics for my organizer, and specific instructions for this are given in the Method section (see also pages 19–21). The dimensions and arrangement for the inside pockets and other holders are all detailed in Fig 17.1.

Method

Before dyeing the fabrics, wash them in a mild detergent, rinse, dry and press.

All lines worked in split stitch

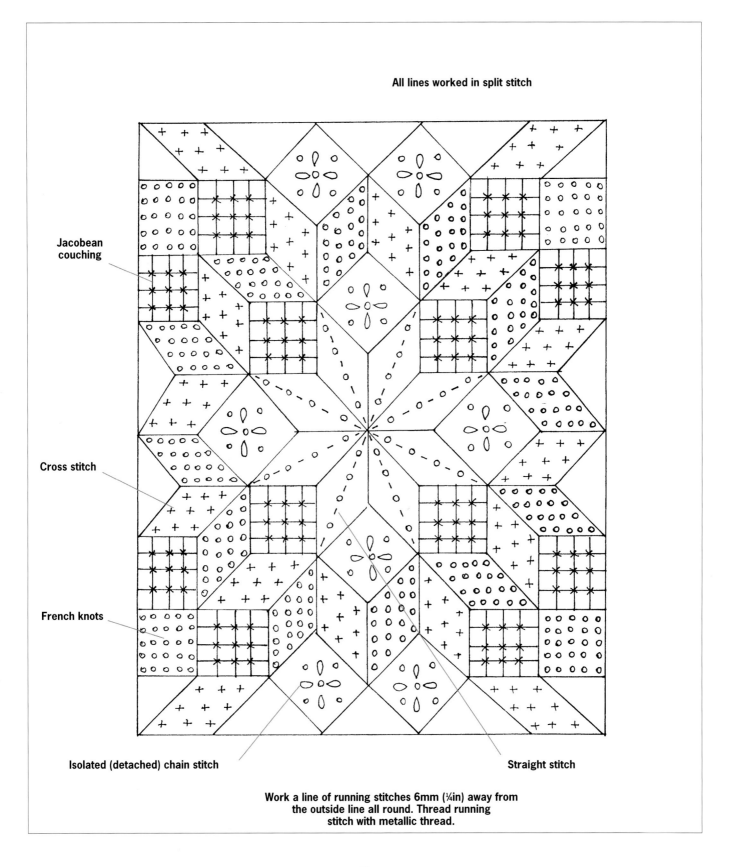

Jacobean couching

Cross stitch

French knots

Isolated (detached) chain stitch

Straight stitch

Work a line of running stitches 6mm (¼in) away from the outside line all round. Thread running stitch with metallic thread.

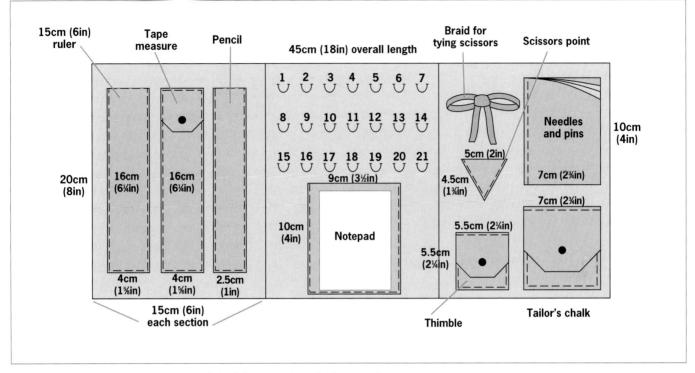

Fig 17.1 Dimensions and arrangement of the different features in the organizer.

Stretch and pin out the main fabric (quilting) with thumbtacks on to a softwood frame as described on page 21. Brush the fabric evenly with cold water, ensuring that it is dampened but not soaking wet (there should be no puddles of water on the surface). With the two dyes of your choice, brush over the fabric to make alternately coloured sections, allowing the dyes to run into each other. Make sure that all the fabric is dyed. Sprinkle the fabric with sea-salt crystals and allow it to dry out naturally. Mark at one corner the right side of the fabric, then remove it from the frame. Rinse the fabric in cold water, dry and then press. Repeat the above process for the plain cotton fabric.

Fold the quilting fabric in half lengthwise and crease, open the fabric out and tack along the crease line. With the right side uppermost, mark three sections on the top portion, each 15cm (6in) wide, with tailor's chalk (see Fig 17.2). The excess fabric all round will be used for turnings. Tack along the tailor's chalk lines. On the top right-hand section, transfer the design centrally, using white or yellow dressmaker's carbon (for dark-coloured dyes), as described on page 15.

On the lower half of the main

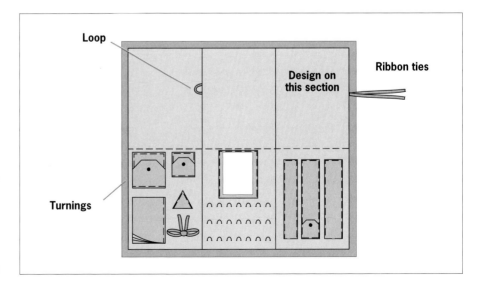

Fig 17.2 Mark the six sections as shown on the right side of the fabric.

fabric and corresponding with the three previously marked sections, mark with tailor's chalk the positions of the pockets and other holders as detailed in Fig 17.1 (see also Fig 17.2).

On the 45cm (17¾in) square piece of plain dyed cotton, mark with tailor's chalk the various items as detailed in Fig 17.1. Allow a 1.5cm (⅝in) turning all round each item. Cut out each piece carefully and tack down all the turnings. Using herringbone stitch, sew down the top hem on the right side of the fabric for the ruler, tape measure, pencil, notepad, scissors, thimble and tailor's chalk sections. Then use herringbone stitch to sew the top, right-hand side and bottom edges for the needle and pin holders, both sides and bottom edges of the flaps for the tailor's chalk, thimble and tape measure.

For the needle and pin holders, cut out three or four pieces of soft fabric (white or cream) slightly smaller than the needle and pin cover. Place these pieces of fabric under the needle and pin cover, and stitch to the cover at the left-hand side only, making sure that they are level.

Pin all the items to the main fabric, aligning all marks. Using herringbone stitch, secure each piece as indicated by the dotted lines in Fig 17.1.

On the middle section, above the notepad holder, mark the positions for the thread tidy (see Fig 17.1). Thread a chenille needle with the narrow ribbon and work loops through the quilting fabric as indicated, ensuring that each loop is secured with back stitches. Place the point of the small embroidery scissors into the point holder and mark the positions for the ribbon which will hold the scissors. Thread the chenille needle with the narrow ribbon and

stitch through the fabric at these marks, ensuring that you leave sufficient ribbon with which to tie the scissors in place.

Stitch two lengths of ribbon (sufficient to tie a bow) on to the centre of the outside edge on the front cover of the needlework organizer. Fold in all the turnings round the outside of the quilting and tack. Fold the fabric over on the central tacked line, matching the corners and the tacking lines. Pin and then tack. Using herringbone stitches, stitch the fabric together around all the edges. Remove all the tacking stitches.

Fold the right-hand section over the middle section, then the left-hand section over the right-hand section. Using the ribbon and a chenille needle, make a small loop to align with the ties on the front cover. Thread the ribbons through the loop and tie.

Chapter Eighteen

Floral Trellis Cushion Cover

MATERIALS

Finished size 41 x 41cm (16 x 16in)

Design area 28 x 28cm (11 x 11in)

Fabric size Front panel: 43 x 43cm (17 x 17in)

Back panel: 2 pieces 43 x 31cm (17 x 12in)

Fabric type 100% linen with slub

WOOL SHADES

(1 skein of each)
Bright rose pink 943, 947
Early English green 541, 543
Heraldic gold 841, 843
Chocolate 186
Bright yellow 551

STITCHES

Stem, satin, closed buttonhole, french knots, detached chain, split

ALTERNATIVE WOOL SHADES

Leaves Grey-green 352, 355

Ribbons and trellis Kingfisher 481, 484

Large flowers Flamingo 621, 623

French knots Flamingo 626

Chain-stitch flowers 621

Small flowers Flesh tints 703, 708

The design for this pretty cushion cover is based on interlinked trellis lines. These are surrounded by decorative flowers and leaves, delicately entwined in an open pattern.

Method

Work this cushion cover and make it up following the instructions given in Chapter 10 for the more traditional floral cushion cover.

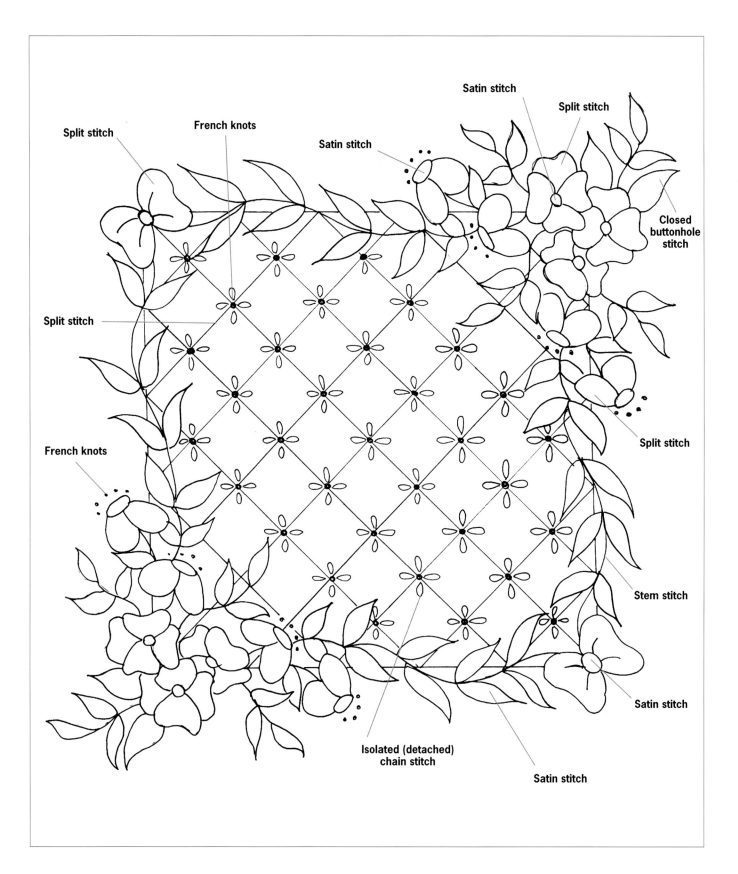

Split stitch

French knots

Satin stitch

Satin stitch

Split stitch

Split stitch

Closed
buttonhole
stitch

Split stitch

French knots

Split stitch

Stem stitch

Isolated (detached)
chain stitch

Satin stitch

Satin stitch

Chapter Nineteen

Galleon Picture

MATERIALS

Finished size 29 x 42cm (11½ x 16½in)

Design area 21 x 29.5cm (8¼ x 11⅝in)

Fabric size Main fabric: 35.5 x 35.5cm (14 x 14in)

Backing fabric: 35.5 x 35.5cm (14 x 14in)

Surround: 50 x 114.5cm (20 x 45in)

Fabric type Main fabric: lightweight silk

Backing fabric: plain, toning cotton

Surround: fabric of contrasting colour and texture

White piping braid 1.5m (1½yd)

Pelmet Vilene 68.5 x 91.5cm (27 x 36in)

Silk dyes White mixer, Turquoise, Ultramarine, Petrol, Grun, Ochre, White outliner, plus outliner tube with metal nozzle point

Sea salt

Paintbrush

WOOL SHADES

(1 skein of each)

Heraldic gold 841

Kingfisher 484

Bright white 991B

Red fawn 304

Leaf green 421, 423

Brown groundings 584

Sea green 401

Orange-red 441

Marine blue 323

Turquoise 525

Metallic silver (Coates OPHIR 301)

Metallic gold (Coates OPHIR 300)

STITCHES

Chain, stem, french knots, split, satin, straight, Jacobean couching

A Turkish galleon with motifs to represent sea and sky forms the design for this project. The embroidery has been worked on silk fabric which has been dyed using the sea salt technique (see page 20).

Method

Place the design on to a clean, flat surface and position the piece of silk fabric over the design. Using masking tape, tape the silk down to the flat surface and lightly draw round the design with a soft pencil. Lift off the

ALTERNATIVE COLOURS

Silk dyes Grey, Turquoise, Ochre, Orange, Sienna, White mixer

Dull the sky and sea by mixing dyes (in small dishes or egg cups) to the required colour. Dye fabric and add touches of brighter shades, toned down with white mixer, to give small hints of extra colour. The overall effect will then be 'moody'. The galleon sails will also need to be toned down with grey.

Wool shades Sea and sky: mixes of Mid blue 151, 154, 156, Turquoise 524, 525, Jacobean green 291A, Grey green 353, Iron grey 961, 963, Bright china blue 741, 743, White 991

French knots: Pastel shades 883

Chain stitch around sails: Iron grey 961

Galleon: Biscuit brown 761, Terracotta 123, 125

---

masking tape and stretch the silk tightly over the dyeing frame (see pages 20–1).

Fit the metal nozzle on to the outliner tube and fill the tube with outliner. Following the red line on the design diagram, gently and carefully use outliner on the silk only over the areas indicated by the red line. Allow the outliner to dry out thoroughly (overnight if possible). Make sure that you empty any leftover outliner back into the bottle and rinse out the tube and nozzle.

On a saucer, mix together a little ochre and white mixer until you have a suitable creamy colour. Paint the sails and ensigns with this, then paint the galleon body with ochre only. Allow to dry.

Paint the sky, mixing ultramarine and white mixer to the colour you require. Use the green, turquoise, petrol and white mixer to paint the sea. Scatter a few of the sea salt crystals on to the sea section only (see page 20) and allow to dry.

Shake off the excess salt and remove the silk from the frame. Immerse the fabric in cold water to remove any salt residue. Once the silk is dry, iron for two minutes on the silk setting.

Tack on a piece of cotton fabric as a backing for the silk. Place the backed silk into a ring frame and work the embroidery stitches. When the embroidery is complete, remove it from the frame and cut a piece of pelmet Vilene to the design size. Tack the silk to the Vilene, turning the excess silk underneath.

Now you will need to space dye the piping braid. Place the braid into cold water, squeeze out the excess water and place the braid on to a sheet of polythene. With the same colours used for dyeing the silk, paint sections of colour along the length of the piping braid. Allow to dry, then tack the piping braid all round the edges of the silk, but avoid stretching the braid. Finish off neatly at one corner.

Now measure and cut another piece of pelmet Vilene 38 x 29cm (15 x 11⅜in). Also cut from the surround fabric a piece measuring 48.5 x 41cm (19 x 16in). Tack the Vilene on to the back of the fabric surround in the position shown in Fig 19.1a. Then turn over the edges on three sides and tack as shown in Fig 19.1b.

Place the fabric surround with its right side uppermost on a flat surface and position the silk embroidery on the fabric surround, right side uppermost, with the silk embroidery about 4cm (1⅝in) from the bottom edge, and allowing about 4cm (1⅝in) down each side. Tack the silk

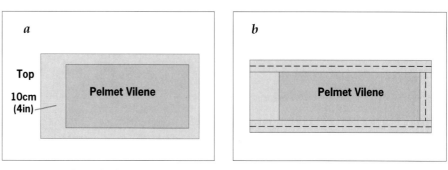

Fig 19.1 Attaching the fabric surround to the pelmet Vilene.

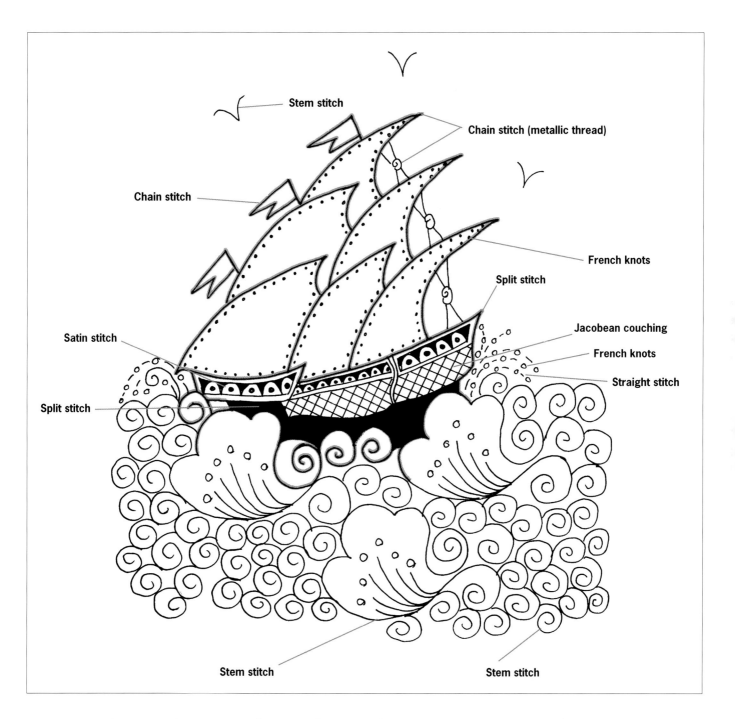

embroidery to the surround.

With small, neat stitches, sew through the piping braid, the silk and the fabric surround, taking care not to pucker or stretch the Vilene. On the top edge of the surround, turn under 1.5cm (⅝in). Fold the top 10cm (4in) in

half on to the back of the work and pin this to the Vilene backing. Sew neatly in place, taking care that the stitches do not show on the right side of the work. The sleeve this hem makes will allow a pole to be threaded through to hang the embroidery.

Cut another piece of fabric from the surround material, approximately 37 x 27cm (14⅝ x 10⅝in). Turn under 1.5cm (⅝in) all round and tack. Place this piece of fabric on to the back of the surround to cover the Vilene and carefully stitch it into place.

Chapter Twenty
Circular Floral Design

MATERIALS

Finished size 30 x 26cm (11¾ x 10in)

Design area 19 x 19cm (7½ x 7½in)

Fabric size 30 x 30cm (11¾ x 11¾in)

Fabric type 100% cream cotton

WOOL SHADES

(1 skein of each)

Hyacinth 891, 892, 895

Leaf green 422, 428

Bright yellow 551

Metallic gold (Coates OPHIR 300)

STITCHES

Detached chain, satin, stem, straight, french knots

ALTERNATIVE WOOL SHADES

Flowers Bright rose pink 941, 944, 947

French knots Wine red 713

Leaves Sea green 401, 402

Flowers Flamingo 622, 623

Leaves Turquoise 522, 525

French knots Flesh tints 705

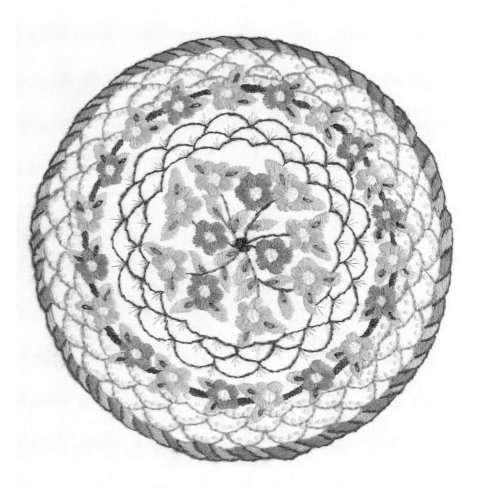

Turkish motifs and embroidery have fascinated me for many years. The flower, sea, sky and leaf motifs can be used to create wonderful patterns and intricate designs as on this flowing, circular design.

Method

Transfer the design centrally on to the fabric as described on pages 14–15. Place the fabric into a ring frame and work the embroidery stitches. When the embroidery is complete, remove it from the ring frame and mount and lace following the instructions given on pages 22–3.

If you fancy a change from square shapes, then a circular cardboard surround or window mount, chosen to tone in with your choice of wool shades, would greatly enhance this design.

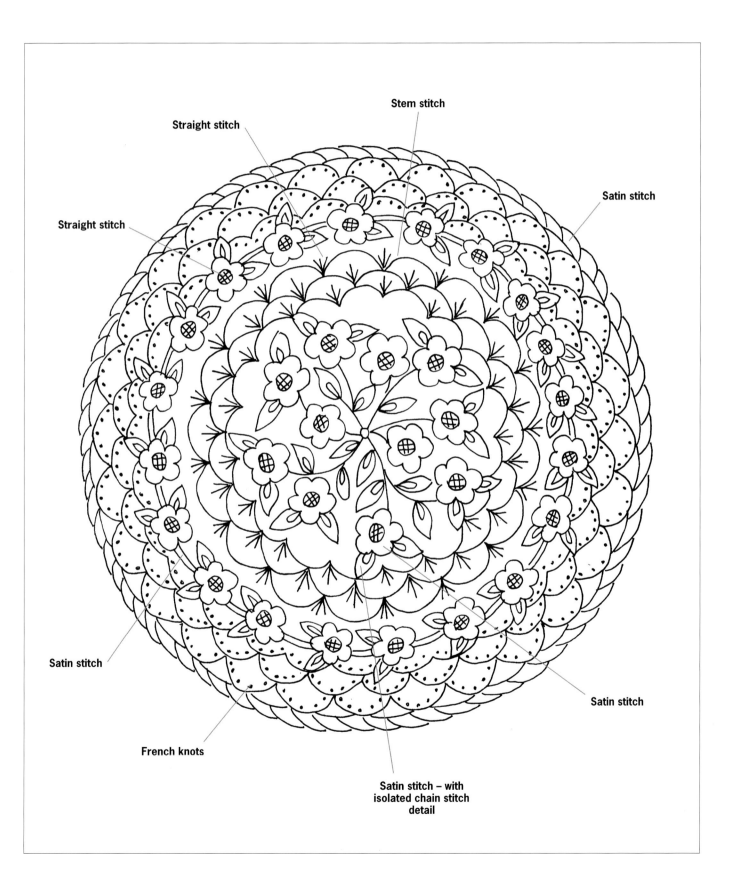

Stem stitch

Straight stitch

Satin stitch

Straight stitch

Satin stitch

Satin stitch

French knots

Satin stitch – with
isolated chain stitch
detail

Chapter Twenty-One

Lid for Ceramic Bowl

MATERIALS

Finished size 9 x 9cm (3½ x 3½in)

Design area 8 x 8cm (3⅛ x 3⅛in)

Fabric size 23 x 23cm (9 x 9in)

Fabric type Zweigart Damask 2168
   Pünktchen 218

WOOL SHADES

(1 skein of each)

Kingfisher 481, 483

Bright yellow 551

Leaf green 422

Metallic gold (Coates OPHIR 300)

STITCHES

Detached chain, straight, french knots,
satin, split

ALTERNATIVE WOOL SHADES

Central flower Bright rose pink 943,
   947

Small chain-stitch flowers Bright rose
   pink 941

Leaves Early English green 541, 543

French knots Bright yellow 551,

Straight stitches Metallic gold

This project is simple and delicate and would be a most acceptable hand-made gift. The ceramic bowls are produced in a variety of colours, sizes and shapes, and may be purchased from most good craft stores.

Method

Transfer the design on to the fabric following the instructions on pages 14–15, then place the fabric into a ring frame and work the embroidery stitches.

Remove the completed work from the ring frame and mount the embroidery inside the ceramic bowl lid, following the instructions given by the manufacturer.

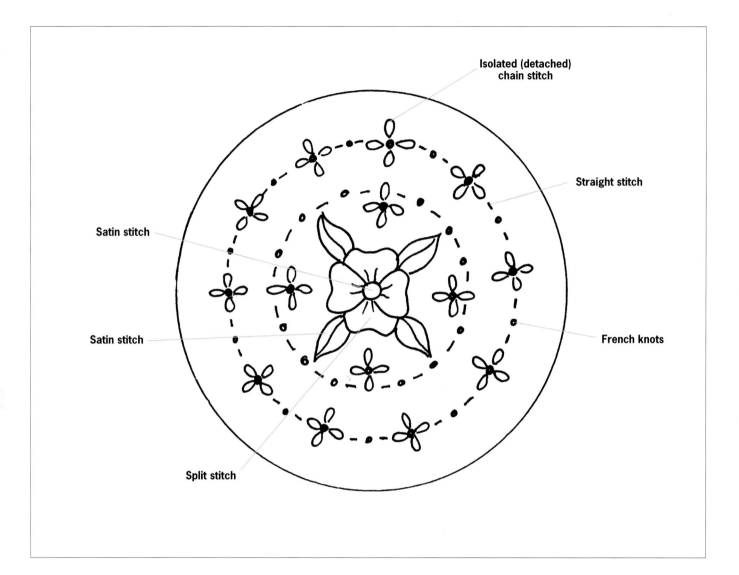

Isolated (detached) chain stitch

Straight stitch

Satin stitch

Satin stitch

French knots

Split stitch

Chapter Twenty-Two

Placemat or Tablecloth

MATERIALS

Finished size of placemat 30 x 37cm
(11¾ x 14⅝in)

Design area 17 x 17cm (6¾ x 6¾in)

Fabric size 34 x 41cm (13⅜ x 16in)

Fabric type
Upper: Zweigart Damask 2168 (55%
cotton/45% rayon) Pünktchen 218
Cream
Lining: Cream cotton/polyester
quilting

WOOL SHADES

(1 skein of each for placemats, 2 or 3 for
tablecloth, depending on size)

Bright china blue 742, 745, 747

Royal blue 821

Autumn yellow 471, 478

Leaf green 421

Early English green 543

Bright rose pink 943

Black 993

Metallic gold (Coates OPHIR 300)

STITCHES

Satin, split, stem, detached chain, french
knots, Jacobean couching

ALTERNATIVE WOOL SHADES

Main flowers Bright mauve 451, 453

Bell flowers Pastel shades 886,
Hyacinth 895

Butterfly Turquoise 523, 525

Leaves Grey-green 353, 355

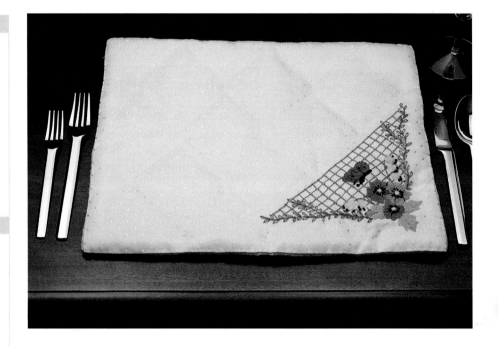

My neighbour's garden is always a riot of colour during the spring and summer months. Garden trellises covered with creeping plants and flowers often attract many species of butterflies, and they provided the inspiration for this project. As well as decorating placemats and a tablecloth, the design could also be used on a set of matching napkins.

Method

Transfer the design on to the main fabric in the bottom right-hand or left-hand corner, ensuring that enough fabric is left around the design area for turnings. Place the design area of the fabric into a ring frame and work the embroidery. When complete, remove the work from the frame and turn under 3cm (1⅛in) all round the edges, tacking the turning in place.

/ / / / / / / / / / / / / / / / / / / /
Tip **The size of the tablecloth will depend entirely on the size of the table it will be covering. See page 78 for proportions.**
/ / / / / / / / / / / / / / / / / / / /

Turn under 2.5cm (1in) all round the edges of the quilting fabric and tack. Place the main fabric (design side uppermost) on to the quilting fabric, ensuring that the edges match. Tack this in place and then, using small back stitches round the edge, join the fabrics together, making sure that the stitches are not visible on the front of the work.

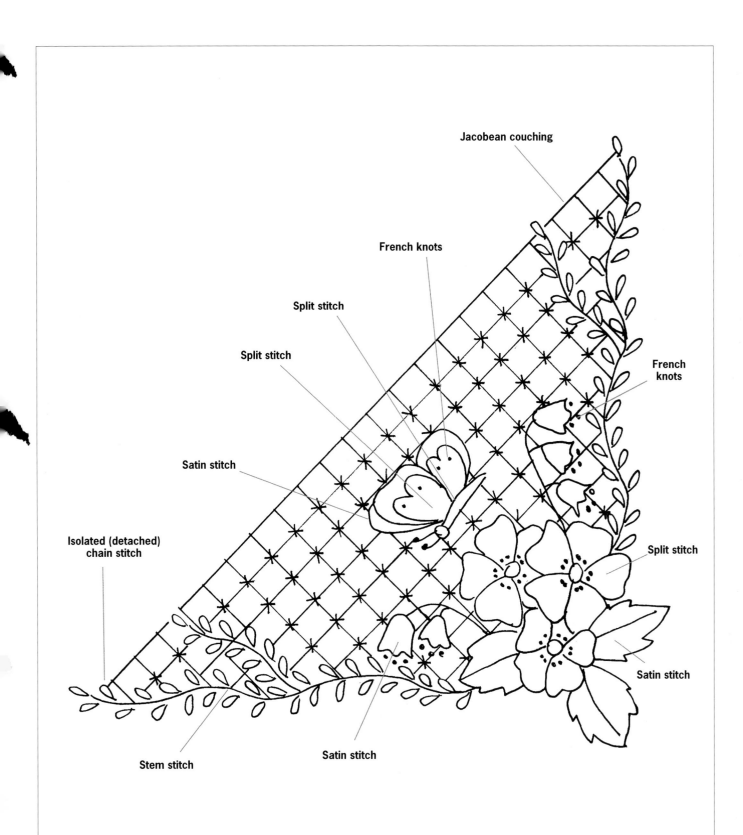

Jacobean couching

French knots

Split stitch

Split stitch

French knots

Satin stitch

Isolated (detached)
chain stitch

Split stitch

Satin stitch

Stem stitch

Satin stitch

Finally, with small, isolated cross stitches, evenly spaced, secure the middle part of the fabrics together as well (see page 39, instructions for padding the spectacle case).

Square or rectangular tablecloth

Measure the table and allow for a 26cm (10in) drop all round. Make a decorated centre panel by first placing the design in the centre and then flipping it by 180°, matching the Jacobean couching areas on the long side (see Fig 22.1a). For the four corners, use the design as it is, but transpose it at opposite ends of the cloth so that the edge with the Jacobean couching faces inwards each time (see Fig 22.1b). You may wish to link up the design areas with Jacobean couching.

Turn up the hems along the edges and machine or slip stitch to finish them off.

Circular or oval tablecloth

Measure the table by placing sheets of newspaper (tape them together to obtain a continuous sheet of the right size) on to the table and creasing the paper to mark the correct shape. Allow a 26cm (10in) drop all round the shape, and cut this out of your fabric.

Work the centre panels as given for the square or rectangular tablecloth. Around the lower edge of the cloth use only the flowers, leaves and butterfly, omitting the Jacobean couching. Turn up the hem all round and machine or slip stitch to finish.

Fig 22.1 The positions of the design for decorating a tablecloth.

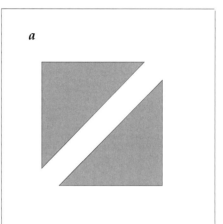

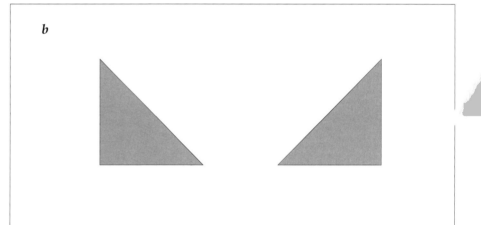

Bibliography

de Denne, Lynette, *Creative Needlecraft*, Sundial
   Publications Ltd, 1979
Jones, Mary Eirwen, *A History of Western Embroidery*,
   Studio Vista Ltd, 1969
Paulson, Christine, *William Morris*, Quantum Books Ltd,
   1989
Snook, Barbara, *English Embroidery*, Mills and Boon, 1960
Swain, Margaret, *The Needlework of Mary Queen of Scots*,
   Van Nostrand Reinhold Co., 1973
Wilson, Erica, *Crewel Embroidery*, Faber and Faber, 1962

Further Reading

Christie, A. G. I., *English Mediaeval Embroidery*, Oxford
   University Press, 1938
Dawson, Pat, *The Art of Painting on Silk*, Search Press,
   1988
Digby, G. W., *Elizabethan Embroidery*, Faber and Faber,
   1963
D.M.C. Library, *Turkish Embroideries*, Editions T. H. de
   Dillmont, Mulhouse (France)
Eaton, Jan, *Mary Thomas's Dictionary of Embroidery
   Stitches*, Hodder & Stoughton, 1989

Metric Conversion Table

inches to millimetres and centimetres
mm = millimetres   cm = centimetres

inches	mm	cm	inches	cm	inches	cm
⅛	3	0.3	9	22.9	30	76.2
¼	6	0.6	10	25.4	31	78.7
⅜	10	1.0	11	27.9	32	81.3
½	13	1.3	12	30.5	33	83.8
⅝	16	1.6	13	33.0	34	86.4
¾	19	1.9	14	35.6	35	88.9
⅞	22	2.2	15	38.1	36	91.4
1	25	2.5	16	40.6	37	94.0
1¼	32	3.2	17	43.2	38	96.5
1½	38	3.8	18	45.7	39	99.1
1¾	44	4.4	19	48.3	40	101.6
2	51	5.1	20	50.8	41	104.1
2½	64	6.4	21	53.3	42	106.7
3	76	7.6	22	55.9	43	109.2
3½	89	8.9	23	58.4	44	111.8
4	102	10.2	24	61.0	45	114.3
4½	114	11.4	25	63.5	46	116.8
5	127	12.7	26	66.0	47	119.4
6	152	15.2	27	68.6	48	121.9
7	178	17.8	28	71.1	49	124.5
8	203	20.3	29	73.7	50	127.0

Index

About the Author

Mavis S Glenny (known to her friends as Mave) is a busy Methodist minister's wife, mother and embroiderer. Mave lives in a small, rugged coastal town on the Ards Peninsula in Northern Ireland. She is a creative needlewoman who has, over the past seven years, taught most forms of embroidery, as well as silk dyeing, fabric painting, appliqué, banner making, patchwork and candlewicking.

Mave has had several pieces exhibited and has given many talks to women's organizations throughout Northern Ireland. She is a member of the Northern Ireland Embroidery Guild and has completed the Creative Embroidery course Parts 1 and 2 with the City and Guilds of London Institute. She is well known in ecclesiastical circles for her banners, pulpit falls and altar frontals, and her work adorns many church sanctuaries, particularly in Ireland.

TITLES AVAILABLE FROM
GMC PUBLICATIONS

BOOKS

WOODWORKING

40 More Woodworking Plans & Projects	GMC Publications
Bird Boxes and Feeders for the Garden	Dave Mackenzie
Complete Woodfinishing	Ian Hosker
David Charlesworth's Furniture-making Techniques	David Charlesworth
Electric Woodwork	Jeremy Broun
Furniture & Cabinetmaking Projects	GMC Publications
Furniture Projects	Rod Wales
Furniture Restoration (Practical Crafts)	Kevin Jan Bonner
Furniture Restoration and Repair for Beginners	Kevin Jan Bonner
Furniture Restoration Workshop	Kevin Jan Bonner
Green Woodwork	Mike Abbott
Making & Modifying Woodworking Tools	Jim Kingshott
Making Chairs and Tables	GMC Publications
Making Fine Furniture	Tom Darby
Making Little Boxes from Wood	John Bennett
Making Shaker Furniture	Barry Jackson
Making Woodwork Aids and Devices	Robert Wearing
Pine Furniture Projects for the Home	Dave Mackenzie
Router Magic: Jigs, Fixtures and Tricks to Unleash your Router's Full Potential	Bill Hylton
Routing for Beginners	Anthony Bailey
The Scrollsaw: Twenty Projects	John Everett
Sharpening Pocket Reference Book	Jim Kingshott
Sharpening: The Complete Guide	Jim Kingshott
Space-Saving Furniture Projects	Dave Mackenzie
Stickmaking: A Complete Course	Andrew Jones & Clive George
Stickmaking Handbook	Andrew Jones & Clive George
Test Reports: The Router and Furniture & Cabinetmaking	GMC Publications
Veneering: A Complete Course	Ian Hosker
Woodfinishing Handbook (Practical Crafts)	Ian Hosker
Woodworking Plans and Projects	GMC Publications
Woodworking with the Router: Professional Router Techniques any Woodworker can Use	Bill Hylton & Fred Matlack
The Workshop	Jim Kingshott

WOODTURNING

Adventures in Woodturning	David Springett
Bert Marsh: Woodturner	Bert Marsh
Bill Jones' Notes from the Turning Shop	Bill Jones
Bill Jones' Further Notes from the Turning Shop	Bill Jones
Colouring Techniques for Woodturners	Jan Sanders
The Craftsman Woodturner	Peter Child
Decorative Techniques for Woodturners	Hilary Bowen
Essential Tips for Woodturners	GMC Publications
Faceplate Turning	GMC Publications
Fun at the Lathe	R.C. Bell
Illustrated Woodturning Techniques	John Hunnex
Intermediate Woodturning Projects	GMC Publications
Keith Rowley's Woodturning Projects	Keith Rowley
Make Money from Woodturning	Ann & Bob Phillips
Multi-Centre Woodturning	Ray Hopper
Pleasure and Profit from Woodturning	Reg Sherwin
Practical Tips for Turners & Carvers	GMC Publications
Practical Tips for Woodturners	GMC Publications
Spindle Turning	GMC Publications
Turning Miniatures in Wood	John Sainsbury
Turning Wooden Toys	Terry Lawrence
Understanding Woodturning	Ann & Bob Phillips
Useful Techniques for Woodturners	GMC Publications
Useful Woodturning Projects	GMC Publications
Woodturning: Bowls, Platters, Hollow Forms, Vases, Vessels, Bottles, Flasks, Tankards, Plates	GMC Publications
Woodturning: A Foundation Course	Keith Rowley
Woodturning: A Source Book of Shapes	John Hunnex
Woodturning Jewellery	Hilary Bowen
Woodturning Masterclass	Tony Boase
Woodturning Techniques	GMC Publications
Woodturning Tools & Equipment Test Reports	GMC Publications
Woodturning Wizardry	David Springett

WOODCARVING

The Art of the Woodcarver	GMC Publications
Carving Birds & Beasts	GMC Publications
Carving on Turning	Chris Pye
Carving Realistic Birds	David Tippey
Decorative Woodcarving	Jeremy Williams
Essential Tips for Woodcarvers	GMC Publications
Essential Woodcarving Techniques	Dick Onians
Lettercarving in Wood: A Practical Course	Chris Pye
Power Tools for Woodcarving	David Tippey
Practical Tips for Turners & Carvers	GMC Publications
Relief Carving in Wood: A Practical Introduction	Chris Pye
Understanding Woodcarving	GMC Publications
Understanding Woodcarving in the Round	GMC Publications
Useful Techniques for Woodcarvers	GMC Publications
Wildfowl Carving - Volume 1	Jim Pearce
Wildfowl Carving - Volume 2	Jim Pearce
The Woodcarvers	GMC Publications
Woodcarving: A Complete Course	Ron Butterfield
Woodcarving: A Foundation Course	Zoë Gertner
Woodcarving for Beginners	GMC Publications
Woodcarving Tools & Equipment Test Reports	GMC Publications
Woodcarving Tools, Materials & Equipment	Chris Pye

UPHOLSTERY

Seat Weaving (Practical Crafts)	Ricky Holdstock
Upholsterer's Pocket Reference Book	David James
Upholstery: A Complete Course (Revised Edition)	David James
Upholstery Restoration	David James
Upholstery Techniques & Projects	David James

TOYMAKING

DOLLS' HOUSES & MINIATURES

CRAFTS

THE HOME & GARDENING

VIDEOS

MAGAZINES

Woodturning • Woodcarving • Furniture & Cabinetmaking • The Dolls' House Magazine
The Router • The ScrollSaw • Creative Crafts for the Home • BusinessMatters • Water Gardening

---

The above represents a full list of all titles currently published or scheduled to be published.
All are available direct from the Publishers or through bookshops, newsagents and specialist retailers.
To place an order, or to obtain a complete catalogue, contact:

GMC Publications
Castle Place, 166 High Street, Lewes, East Sussex BN7 1XU, United Kingdom   Tel: 01273 488005 Fax: 01273 478606

Orders by credit card are accepted